THE
BOOK O

Christopher Floris

THE FLORIS
BOOK OF
CAKES

André Deutsch

First published 1981 by
André Deutsch Limited
105 Great Russell Street London WC1

British Library Cataloguing in Publication Data
Floris, Christopher
    The Floris book of cakes.
    1. Cake
    1. Title   11. Book of cakes
    641.8′653   TX771

    ISBN 0–233–96978–0

Printed in Great Britain by
Ebenezer Baylis and Son Ltd
The Trinity Press, Worcester, and London

Contents

List of Illustrations

Acknowledge-ments

It was once suggested to me that I should try and write my autobiography. I haven't and won't – partly because I've never managed to keep a diary beyond about January 10, partly because if I did write it I would write the truth as I saw it and that might upset some people and partly because I am lazy but *mainly* because the only person who would be likely to want to read it is me – and I'm not even sure about that!

However, if I were to try and acknowledge everyone who has helped me in one way or another with this book I would come very near to writing the story of my life. For I have been very lucky. I have met many kind and interesting people. I have been to many beautiful and exciting places. I have worked with people who must be among the 'greats' of our trade. To all those I am grateful. A few must be mentioned by name:—

Marjorie Josephs, while coping with the preparations for her son's wedding, managed to decipher my extraordinary handwriting and prepared the typescript. Sheila Toussaint, who while repapering her bathroom with one hand, laying a carpet with the other and mastering the intricacies of clutch and accelerator with her feet, somehow found the time to give invaluable help with the research and compilation of this book. My wonderful colleagues Elizabeth Halls, Derek Hayes and Charles Smith, who encouraged and advised me and then read the typescript. My editor, Esther Whitby, with whom I fought amicably, cheerfully and, for me entertainingly, over matters of style and intelligibility. Last but not least, my compatriot and publisher, André Deutsch, who showed patience that is wholly untypical in a Hungarian. If this book is considered to have any merit, the lion's share of it must go to them. The faults are my own.

Preface

I was born in Budapest in 1926. My very first girl friend was born some three weeks after I was (why is it that girls so often arrive late, even for their first date with a man?) At first our prams were pushed along side by side; in due course we toddled together and eventually played. It was an odd sort of friendship – I do assure you we were 'just good friends' – because her father was a director of a bank while my parents made chocolates and cakes. In the social scale of those unspeakably snobbish days she was much grander than I.

Inevitably the day came when we had our first quarrel. I cannot now remember what it was that I had done to arouse her wrath, but there can be no doubt that arouse it I did. She turned on me with that mixture of fury and dignity that can be found only in a little girl of four or five and, searching her vocabulary for the nastiest name she could call me, said 'You – you – you pastry cook!'

A couple of decades later, in England, I was invited to the home of a very eminent doctor who had a number of unmarried daughters to dispose of. Most of the young gentlemen present were either medical students or recently qualified doctors or surgeons from my distinguished host's hospital. I asked a young lady to dance (I never did find out if she was one of the daughters on display) and by way of scintillating conversation she asked me, 'Are you at St ——'s Hospital?' 'No,' I said, 'I fear I am not.' 'Oh,' she replied, 'you're in private practice then.' 'No,' I told her, 'I'm afraid I'm not medical at all.' 'You're not?' Incredulity clouded her otherwise vacant expression, 'What are you then?' 'I'm a baker.'

The rest of that evening passed uneventfully. I struck up a pleasant but not lasting friendship with one of the barmen and eventually had an invigorating, though solitary, walk home.

The points of those two anecdotes are that I was born into the baking trade and that I have never felt any need to be ashamed of it. I might add that they also give a hint of my mother's determined and persistent efforts to launch me into Society – efforts that were resisted, with matching determination and persistence, by both Society and me.

Having spent quite a long time in and around the bakery trade, I approached this book with some trepidation. Things that can be done in a commercial bakery cannot necessarily be done in a domestic kitchen and vice versa. This is especially so because most bakeries have been designed, with greater or lesser success, for the purpose for which they are used while in most modern houses the kitchen seems to me to have been treated as an unimportant afterthought. I suppose I ought now to apologise to any architect into whose hands this book may fall and I will willingly do so in exchange for his promise to remember in future designs that the kitchen is a workshop, a laboratory, a social centre and the place where the cook of the household (mother, father, son, daughter, spinster or bachelor) will spend a substantial proportion of every day.

Cooking in general and baking in particular is an art, a science, a dedication and a joy. In these inflationary days it may be that home baking is economical, though frankly I doubt it. The commercial pastry cook has more and better equipment, can buy materials more cheaply, can plan production more economically and, in terms of percentage, has less waste. On the other hand, in these days of dying craftsmanship, it could be that home baking generally produces higher quality. For obvious reasons I must be hesitant about commenting. I will say only that while the best of commercially made cakes, pastries and bread are excellent, there are some on the market that are of very poor quality indeed. Yet even these are sold, and sold in sizeable quantities.

If then neither price nor quality furnish a reason for home cake and bread making, what reason remains? Why has this book been written? Cakes and bread – you will see that I have not been able to resist slipping in a few *bread* recipes right at the end – are easily available but there are some things that cannot be bought and those are the satisfaction, the pleasure, the fun of creating. That is why this book came into being and that, I hope, is why it is being read.

I have included some ideas about the equipment and others on buying your ingredients. Among the equipment are courage, dedication and patience. Among the ingredients, and first among them, is your heart.

So, let's go into the kitchen together, we may both learn something.

Horsted Keynes
Sussex

Before We Begin

Kitchen

No one has ever designed a kitchen with too much storage space. Cupboards are needed for the storage of tools (pots and pans, knives, whisks, etc.) and equipment (electric mixer, scales, etc.) for raw materials, both 'dry' and 'wet', for tinned items, perishable items, for your finished cakes, biscuits and bread, for your cleaning materials and so on. Every last millimetre of your kitchen should be functional. In many kitchens too many corners are wasted. Every cupboard, every shelf, every drawer should be designed for its purpose. Many manufacturers of kitchen furniture have produced excellent items to meet all, or nearly all, these requirements. Among the best, in my view, is the Hygena range (see author's note page 22).

Before you spend any money at all on re-styling your kitchen, sit down and draw up a list of all the things you plan to do in it and make sure you haven't forgotten anything. When this is done make another list of what you will need to make these activities as simple and painless as possible. (All cooking is liable to make you warm. There is no point in getting hot and bothered as well!) Check this second list even more carefully. You will certainly need an oven, a hob (see page 19) and a refrigerator (see page 20) but everyone must decide for themselves which of the other appliances, like washing machines, dishwashers and rotary irons they want to have. Relate all these with the space you have available (too small, isn't it?) and then write to Hygena, or perhaps some other firm, and get their suggestions.

Now, a few things to bear in mind when you plan your kitchen:

——If at all possible, have a strong, wooden-topped table in the centre of the room, but make sure it doesn't make free movement difficult or impossible.

——The floor should be hard wearing and easy to clean and, like all else in the kitchen, pleasing to the eye. Amtico floor tiles, though certainly not the cheapest, are in my view the best value for money for the purpose.

——An extractor fan is just about essential. You do not want to work in a steamy atmosphere, you do not want the smell of your excellent steak and kidney pie to affect your Gâteau St Honoré and you can't afford a through draught. That you might get a severe cold does not really matter; you will at least recover. Your bread dough will not!

——Last, but not least, have a chair in the kitchen – after all, you deserve a cup of coffee from time to time. I suggest *one* chair, but you may like to have several. My kitchen is my workshop, my laboratory, my studio, my sanctum sanctorum. I'd love to sit down and have a chat, but why not wait for me in the sitting-room, I won't be long!

Some last words on kitchen layout: make it as labour and movement saving as possible. Remember, for example, that the average three course meal will produce about thirteen items per person to be washed up and every item of washing up involves at least five separate functions. For a family of four that means 260 movements per meal, assuming 344 such meals a year (I am giving you three weeks holiday!) that means 89,440 per year. If you have a long and happy family life, and I pray that you do, this number may be multiplied by fifty and that gives a grand total of just under four and a half million! A saving of only ten per cent is worth achieving and I am prepared to bet that in most kitchens much more could be accomplished.

I will not attempt here a list of all that you could have in your kitchen. I will just suggest those things you should have to make baking the joy that it can be.

Equipment

The amount of equipment, tools and gadgets you can have in your kitchen is endless. There can be few days when some new and 'indispensable' bit of ironmongery, or plasticmongery, does not hit the market. There are almost as many days on which such items disappear again. The only limits need be the size of your kitchen and the capacity of your pocket. A little common sense, however, can do no harm. Avoid those very special gadgets that take up space and serve only one rare purpose. That marvellous, computerised, transistorised, all electric (special adaptor for use with North Sea Gas £8.50 extra), chromium-plated, high-speed late-night snack dispenser is not quite so high-speed when it has taken you an hour to find it, another hour to clean it, a third to mend a broken connection and fit a new plug and a fourth to read and understand the instructions (translated from Sanskrit by a Peruvian ornithologist)! Similarly, I am inclined to doubt the real efficacy of that new multi-purpose time saver which will roll out pastry while it is percolating coffee, simultaneously playing extracts from the Nutcracker Suite and giving you a massage or shave (tooth polisher optional extra).

Equip your kitchen with the best tools and equipment you can afford. This will often mean the simplest and most durable. The best is not cheap, but the cheapest can prove to be expensive. Buy a little at a time and make a life-long pastime of equipping your kitchen – it is a pleasant and worthwhile occupation.

When you have some tools and equipment, take care of them. A good kitchen knife makes a rotten screwdriver. As far as possible wash or otherwise clean every item as you finish with it or, if you can get away with it, get someone else to do it for you.

Make your kitchen a happy place. Treat it with love and it will respond.

The list of items that follows is in alphabetical order:

APPLE CORER

The simple, old-fashioned design has not been substantially improved on.

BAKING TINS

There are a great many sizes and shapes available. If you are making bread you may want to bake it in bread tins from 1 lb (500 g) upwards. Personally, I prefer bread baked on trays or the oven bottom, but these bread tins are useful for certain cakes as well. For cakes you will need a selection of round baking tins, ranging from 7″ (15 cm) to, say, 9″ (22 cm) in diameter and from 1″ (2.5 cm) to 3″ (8 cm) in depth. Again, Tower non-stick tins will save you time and trouble.

BAKING TRAYS

Have several of these. They should be as big as will fit into your oven but not less than 11″ × 16″ (20 cm × 30 cm). Tower brand, among others, make excellent baking trays with non-stick surfaces. These need little or no preparation (greasing or lining) and properly treated will last a very long time. Baking trays with special indentations for buns, sponge fingers, etc., are available but are worth getting only if you are going to make a great many of the items in question.

BOWLS

It is almost impossible to have too many. Lots of different sizes are available. If you intend to make bread as well as cakes you should, ideally, have at least one large wooden bowl for proving the dough.

CLOCK

A reliable, easy-to-read, clock is essential. If you can get one with a 'minute pinger' so much the better.

CLOTHS

You will need several serviceable linen or cotton cloths. Doughs that need to prove must be covered, swiss rolls need to be rolled. These cloths never get really dirty but must always be rinsed out and properly dried after each use. A number of excellent pastry cooks suggest using polythene sheets instead of cloths but though such sheets are easy to use and clean for some reason I have never been happy with them.

CONTAINERS

Flour, sultanas, sugar, etc. are all sold in packages

to return. Apart from that, it can also be used as a coffee grinder, and you deserve a decent cup of coffee. The Kenwood Chef Mixer has an attachment that is just right.

NIVES

A small pointed knife, a large butcher's knife, a paring knife, a palette knife (make sure it is flexible), a chopping knife, a bread knife – the list is endless. You will not find better than tempered steel 'French' knives like those made by Sabatier. They are *not* stainless and must, therefore, be cleaned and dried properly.

NIFE RACK

If knives are not sharp they are useless. If they are sharp they can be dangerous. The place *not* to keep knives is loose in a drawer. They will lose their edge and you are bound to cut yourself. Have a knife rack, either in a drawer or on the wall. The wall fittings that I like best are the magnetic ones.

NIFE SHARPENER

If knives are not sharp, I repeat, they are useless. A 'steel' is very useful if you have the special knack of using one. Otherwise a good electric knife sharpener is a must.

IXER

Some say an electric mixer is a luxury but in my opinion a good, versatile one is essential. There are very many on the market. I cannot say that I have tried them all but I have tried a large number and my choice is the Kenwood Chef. Not only has it a huge selection of useful attachments but its range of speeds is very wide indeed. In my opinion it would be better still if its slowest speed was somewhat slower, but it is still my favourite. Although I do not specify using an electric mixer in any of the recipes you will find that with the right mixer all mixing, kneading, blending and whisking is much quicker and easier. As a general principle always start at the slowest speed and increase it, a little at a time, until you achieve the result you want. To no small extent this must, in early days, be a question of trial and error.

of different sizes and shapes. An
investments was a number of t
tainers (I got them at Woolwortl
neat and, being transparent, I can
nearly out of this or that when
shopping list.

K

COOLING RACK

A wire mesh tray with legs. The
grill will probably serve. You need
probably more.

CUPS

Those cups that have had the handl
have a small but unsightly chip or l
from Niggling-on-Sea' emblazon
(unless that was a very special w
should not be thrown away but u
small quantities of raw materials, s
marking out smallish rings and, w
them really well, for measuring su
Do *not* save cracked cups for thi
purpose. The only place for crack
dustbin.

K

FIRST AID KIT

I know you are careful but it's be
safe side. One day your cat may trip
has often tripped me . . .

M

FORKS

One or two 'dinner' sized stainless
be useful. It would be a pity to use
priceless canteen of solid silver cu
given as a wedding present. You ma
they were only silver plated!

GRATER

A good, sturdy, three or four sid
different gauges and types of edge
able not only for pastry cookery
cookery as well.

GRINDER

A good, simple, electric grinder wi
its keep. Ground nuts are needed in
and it is always better to grind you
you buy may be past the first flush
some of the flavour-giving oils will ha

MOULDS

From small jam tart moulds to large jelly moulds, these are always useful. Whenever you see any interesting moulds and can afford them, get them. Once you have your moulds treat them as you treat your toothbrush, your pen or your spouse — *don't lend them*!

OVEN AND HOB

Let me assume that you are in a position to restyle your kitchen completely and that you intend to do a lot of baking. An eye-level double oven (upper and lower) with a glass door inside the main door and a light inside the oven is not merely ostentatiously extravagant, it will save your back and, because of the inner door and light, you will be able to inspect the progress of your handiwork without reducing the heat of the oven too often. Even so, open the oven door as seldom as possible. The hob should have not less than four rings or burners and, ideally, should be set flush into one of your kitchen units. My own choice is the 'Tricity' oven by Thorn Electric.

OVEN GLOVES

Either get these or a much larger First Aid kit!

PAPER (GREASEPROOF)

This is essential for lining trays and tins other than 'non-stick' ones, but even if you have non-stick ware you should wrap plain cakes and sponges before storing them (but only when they are properly cool). You will also need greaseproof paper for piping bags.

PASTRY BOARD

An old, warped, stained, splintering bit of plywood will *not* do. A proper, purpose made board is necessary.

PASTRY BRUSH

Quality is vital. Would you or your guests be the more embarrassed when they need to pick bristles out of their mouths?

PASTRY CUTTERS

Get as large and varied a set as you yearn for and your purse will allow. Metal ones usually give a better cut, but you will need to be careful not to bend or dent them. Plastic ones are easier to clean but tend to be brittle and less sharp.

PEELERS

For apples, potatoes, etc. Again the old-fashioned design cannot be bettered. There are some on the market suitable for left or right-handed use, which is useful if two people are to use the kitchen only one of whom is left handed or if, like Walter Mitty, you are ambidexterous.

PIPING BAGS

Good quality canvas or plastic 'Savoy' bags, thin but strong, should be available at your nearest kitchen supply shop. There are metal piping syringes available but I find them a little bit too small and thus awkward to use.

PIPING TUBES

The nozzles that fit to the end of the piping bags are called 'tubes' and no one who is interested in pastry cooking as a trade or a hobby can have too large a selection of these. Start with just one or two and add to them. Your collection, if carefully bought and properly treated, could become an heirloom.

PLATES

Odd plates are useful in the same way as odd cups. Here again the odd chip on the outside doesn't matter but cracked plates should be thrown away.

REFRIGERATOR

No firm can afford to make an inefficient refrigerator. The range of sizes, shapes, capacities, etc. is enormous. Pick one to suit and fit your kitchen. My own choice would be Kelvinator.

ROLLING PIN

A piece off an old broom handle or an empty milk bottle may be all right in an emergency, but not as a regular tool. The best rolling pins work on a spindle so that the handles stay still while the rest rotates.

SAUCEPANS

I'm sure I don't have to explain the importance of a good selection of saucepans. Again Tower or some other good quality non-stick pan will save you a lot of time and trouble.

SCALES

A good, sturdy, easy-to-clean set of scales is, of course, essential. Don't get obsessional about this.

You do not need scales with the accuracy of a chemist's.

SIEVES

A fine sieve is very important. Despite what the advertisements tell you, I still maintain that sifting your own flour is worthwhile. You should make a habit of it. The best miller in the world can make a mistake and the odd lump may form. Also it is not impossible for some 'foreign matter' to find its way into your bag of flour. I do not imply that either the mill or your kitchen is not one hundred per cent hygienic, but accidents can always happen where people are involved.

SPATULAS

These may be wooden, metal, plastic or rubber. You will be using a spatula to help you in mixing your paste or dough by bringing the bits stuck around the edge of your bowl to the centre, to scrape up any stray bits of paste or dough off your pastry board and to scrape out your bowl — you don't want to waste any of that marvellous mixture you have made! Because of the many uses of a spatula I like mine to be slightly flexible and therefore I don't favour wooden ones. A friend of mine scrapes his bowls with a piece of cardboard. I disapprove of this because I am sure some cardboard is bound to find its way into the paste but, as if to annoy me, he always makes the most marvellous pastries and cakes with never a hint of cardboard about them.

SPOONS

All that I said about forks applies to spoons, only more so.

TABLE BRUSH

You can't work properly in a mess. After every phase of the recipe you will need to clean your working surface. Flour, sugar, bits of fruit, etc. must be cleared away. A good whitewashing brush will serve very well — as long as it is never actually used for whitewashing!

THERMOMETER

Eventually, as you get more ambitious, you will need a reliable sugar thermometer. Meanwhile the sight of it may impress some of your friends. Others, perhaps, will just think you a show-off. And if you have a sugar thermometer (or any other piece of equipment) that you do not use, they are right.

TURNTABLE

A simple turntable will save you a lot of irritation and effort when finishing gâteaux or decorating cakes.

WHISK

Even if you have an electric mixer a good, sturdy whisk will be invaluable for whisking up small quantities or for use whilst something is actually heating. A cheap whisk will soon drive you mad.

WOODEN SPOONS

I have never seen a kitchen with too many wooden spoons. Apart from anything else they look nice.

NOTE: In discussing furniture, tools and equipment for your kitchen I have mentioned certain brand names. I have done this because I have often been asked which tools I prefer and have therefore given the matter some thought. I have not been offered (nor have I asked for) any sort of inducement to mention one make in preference to another. The makes I mention do no more than indicate my own taste and I certainly have no intention of implying that there is anything wrong with the makes I do not mention by name.

Preparation

Let us assume that it is Sunday and that you have invited some friends to dinner for next Friday. The magnificent meal that you are planning to serve includes a number of items that you intend to bake.

Decide as soon as possible what you are going to make and read the recipes through carefully. No later than Tuesday evening check your kitchen to make sure that you have all the raw materials you will need and that the necessary equipment is clean and in working order. Any items that you need you can shop for on Wednesday and Thursday morning.

Unless you last baked very recently you ought to need flour – I cannot stress too often that it is *not* good policy to keep large quantities of flour at home. It will probably be wise to start your baking on Thursday leaving Friday clear for the rest of your cooking and, if you are making a gâteau, to fill and finish it.

If you are planning one of the celebration cakes it may be just as well to have it finished by Wednesday evening or Thursday morning. When your guests are due in half an hour and you haven't washed or changed is no time to be decorating a birthday cake!

Before you actually start baking check through the recipe again. When you have read *all through it*, lay out the materials you are going to need – as far as possible in the order that you are going to use them – and also lay out your tools and equipment so that every piece of it is ready to hand. Prepare your tins or mould by greasing them with melted butter (a rub around with a discarded butter wrapper is an easy and effective way) and line with greaseproof paper cut to size. Even with non-stick pans it's a good idea to line the base. Have one or two bowls of hot water by you, in which you can put any items that need washing, or have the sink filled with hot water – or both. Now, if you are appropriately and comfortably dressed, wash your hands and begin. I know that some television cooks perform dressed as if they were attending a Court reception in Imperial Russia, but a kitchen is a place for hard, creative, enjoyable work, not for parlour tricks and cabaret acts.

It is to help you with the preparation that I have set out all the recipes giving you first the ingredients you will need, then the equipment to have ready, next the temperature at which to set the oven and finally the method.

The first thing to do is light and set your oven. You have, of course, remembered that the oven is one of the items of equipment that needs to be spotlessly clean – the smell of burnt oven dirt does nothing to improve the taste of your baking and, just as important, a dirty oven is inefficient and unreliable.

Those of you who are brilliant mathematicians or have recently been given an electronic calculator may notice that the metric weights and measurements I give do not always accord exactly with the old-style equivalents. The fact of the matter is that in the first place your kitchen scales are not that accurate – unless you have quite unnecessarily equipped yourself with something very elaborate – and in the second place the variations in the quality of the materials you buy make certain tolerances unavoidable. Anyway, I bet you never weigh anything to the nearest quarter ounce. Baking is a science and an art and that is another way of saying that it is a science in which artistic licence is permitted. That does not mean that you should ignore the quantities I have so painstakingly worked out for you but it does mean that minor variations are not only permissible but may be essential. I cannot tell you when they will be required – only experience can do that.

Among the recipes you will find some that are fairly well known and others that are less familiar and tend towards the exotic. I have not given any *simple* cake recipes. Nor has anyone else. There is no such thing. Let me explain, before you give the idea of baking up in despair. Some years ago at a dinner given for and by La Confrèrie de la Chaîne des Rôtisseurs (a splendid organisation dating back to the year 1248 and devoted to the appreciation of good food), a few of us discussed what one dish we would set a cook to test him. It was not a long discussion. We quickly agreed that the dish would be scrambled eggs. We felt that if a cook can produce good scrambled eggs then there is a good chance that he would do well with other dishes too. If he were to treat scrambled eggs with contempt, then he was not worthy of anyone's respect – at least, not ours. What I am driving at is that there is no dish, cake, confection or other item of cookery that deserves less care than any other. From that it must follow that none deserves more. If you are not in the mood to give of your best and it is not absolutely vital that you should cook or bake, then leave it to another time, another day, another year. I have said that the most important ingredient in all the recipes in the world is your heart. How can you hope to create a successful dish if the most important ingredient has been left out?

Some Hints on Materials

FLOUR

I have not suggested using self-raising flour in any of the recipes. I find it is easier to make my own by adding baking powder or bicarbonate of soda. It means not only that I can control the amount of 'self-raising' but also that I do not need to have two packets of flour in my cupboard where one would do. Of course, if you happen to have one of those seven acre kitchens I see pictures of in glossy magazines, that's different, but tell me, how do you remember which of all those cupboards the flour is in?

SUGAR

Caster sugar is the most useful sugar in cake making. It seems to mix more easily. If you can get hold of a couple of vanilla pods to keep in your sugar container with the sugar, so much the better.

FAT

Where butter is called for a good, fresh, unsalted butter is the best. It is always possible to add salt to a mixture but to get it out again is impossible. However, for many recipes, margarine or pure lard are not only permissible, they are actually better. Do not overstock your kitchen with fats; they do not improve with age and, needless to say, keep what stock you do have in your refrigerator.

EGGS

Always break eggs into a cup, one at a time, before adding them to anything. The most reliable shop in the world may occasionally supply a bad one and any cook knows just how unpleasant that can be!

YEAST

Yeast is a living organism and should, in my view, be fresh. If you are obliged to use 'dried' yeast, you will find directions for its use on the packet. But try to avoid this. I am convinced that fresh yeast gives better results and all references to yeast in the recipes that follow are to the fresh version.

DRIED FRUIT

Keeping dried fruits too long may cause the sugar in them to crystallise and they will become hard and taste of nothing else. What you do have in stock should be kept clean, dry and in as near to air-tight a container as possible. The paper or cellophane bag they come in will not do for more than a day or two after it has been opened.

CHOCOLATE

The traditional and best way to add chocolate flavour to a mixing of any kind – cake or filling – is to buy plain, unsweetened chocolate – if you can get it – melt it down very carefully over a low heat and pour in the molten chocolate. Do not, as many have tried, attempt to thin the chocolate down with water – this will turn it into a rather nasty, puddingy, mess. If you can't get hold of unsweetened chocolate Bournville's, which is only slightly sweetened, will do. As for the terms 'plain', 'bitter' and 'semi-sweet' which occur in the recipes: 'plain' means *not* milk; 'bitter' advertises itself as such and 'semi-sweet' is good old Bournville's 'plain'. The easiest way to add chocolate flavour is to sprinkle a good quality cocoa powder into the mixture.

COFFEE

The old-fashioned way to add coffee flavour is to make some very strong, freshly ground coffee – using about three times the coffee you would normally use or, alternatively, about one third of the water. The easier way is to add instant coffee powder which should be dissolved where there is liquid in the recipe, otherwise sieved in with the dry ingredients. Granules must always be dissolved and aren't as useful.

COLOURS

Colours are not alway easy to find. Try if you can to get pure vegetable colours rather than synthetic ones. Add these to your mixture a very little at a time – they are usually stronger than you think. Mix the colour in until it is evenly spread through the mixture before you make up your mind to add any more. Far be it from me to dictate to you on matters of taste, but I feel that delicate, pastel shades are more appetising than very vivid colours.

FLAVOURS

The correct thing to do is to make your own – in the case of fruit flavours, fruit pulp, carefully sieved and reduced. But this is not always possible. You can buy concentrates. Try and get these and things like pure almond oil or peppermint oil rather than essences. Be very, very careful using them – just a drop, or a tenth of a drop at a time – and mix thoroughly and keep tasting.

Getting It All Together

In the recipes you will notice that different words are used on different occasions to describe the process of adding one thing to another. The various expressions are, in a sense, describing different 'gears'. I attempt here an explanation of the most commonly used ones, though most pastry cooks have their own, private understanding of these words.

SIEVE TOGETHER

Flour *always*, and other dry powdered materials almost always, needs to be sieved. If two or more such materials are to be added to the recipe at the same time, the most efficient and time-saving method of mixing them is to put them in the sieve at the same time. This way you are not only sieving any lumps or impurities out but the activity of sieving does most of the mixing for you.

FOLD

The term is in itself descriptive. It usually applies to adding something – flour or another mixing – to whipped cream or whisked egg whites. If this is done without care the effort that has gone into whipping or whisking may be wasted and, even worse, the materials too, as it is just about impossible to resurrect whipped cream or whisked egg whites that have collapsed – 'fallen back'. So to 'fold in' means just that: add the new ingredient or mixing to the whipped one slowly, and with a spatula gently fold them over and over together until they unite and live happily ever after!

BLEND AND STIR

These are almost the same and mean moving a whisk, spoon or spatula gently and steadily round and round in the mixing until all of the ingredients are inseparable. Blending is gentler than stirring.

MIX

This means putting two or more ingredients, dry or wet, together so that all of them are evenly distributed within the mixing.

CREAM

Converting sugar and butter or sugar and egg or some other such combination – nearly always involving sugar – into a slightly viscous creamy consistency by firm and steady (*not* violent) agitation with a whisk or fork. This is called creaming together, for obvious reasons.

BEAT

This is vigorous mixing. It affects not only the distribution of the ingredients but also their interaction. Beating affects the texture of the mixing – e.g. beat to a creamy texture.

WHISK AND WHIP

You whisk eggs and whip cream. This is wholly to achieve the desired texture. The implement is a good wire whisk; the movement is a fairly rapid rotation of the whisk; the object is to achieve a thickening and stiffening of the material. Timing is vital: tire too soon and you achieve nothing, carry on too long and it all collapses or 'falls back'. Adding a little caster sugar will help with cream and a pinch of salt will do the same for egg whites.

TEST FOR READINESS   To test a cake for readiness, press it lightly in the centre. If you leave a dent, give it a little longer. The cake is ready when it springs back into place.

NOTE: All these processes can be done with an electric mixer but you must keep a careful check on the speed as all mixers, even the Kenwood Chef, start at a rather brisker speed than I would like. So start at the slowest speed and increase it, only very gradually. With some mixes if you try and save time by putting the mixer at too high a speed too soon, you may well find that will you have to spend the next week redecorating your kitchen!

Weights, Measures, Times and Temperatures

Some readers will notice that I am not always absolutely consistent in giving weights and measurements and that I use 'about' a good deal. They will notice particularly that the conversions to metric denominations are not perfectly accurate. This should not bother you. The point is, as I keep on saying and will continue to say, the variables in cooking are so many that the resulting permutations are infinite. Raw materials, ovens, ambient temperature and humidity are seldom the same twice. Even the temperature of your hands can make a difference. Above all – as if you didn't know – tastes vary. What is more, normal kitchen scales are not accurate to the nearest milligram and there is no reason why they should be. I very much doubt if the temperature setting on your oven is accurate to the last degree either. Common sense, tempered by experience, will adjust my vagueness to the accuracy you want.

Last Minute Reminders

Remember that FLOUR MUST ALWAYS BE SIEVED though I don't repeat this instruction every time.

Remember that flour means PLAIN FLOUR and either proprietary baking powder or bicarbonate of soda may be used as a raising agent. For simplicity's sake I refer simply to BAKING POWDER.

Remember that yeasts means FRESH YEAST – the fresher the better, and butter means UNSALTED BUTTER – always preferable in cake making.

Remember that COFFEE GRANULES (unlike coffee powder) must always be dissolved before use and that PLAIN CHOCOLATE may be used for UNSWEETENED CHOCOLATE which can be hard to find.

Remember that it's always a good idea to WASH DRIED FRUIT. Currants, raisins and sultanas, even from the best suppliers, have a fair bit of grit about them.

Remember that CAKE TINS AND MOULDS MUST ALWAYS BE GREASED OR LINED.

Remember to HAVE ALL YOUR EQUIPMENT READY and, most important of all, to PRE-SET YOUR OVEN and LINE UP ALL YOUR INGREDIENTS before you begin.

Plain Cakes, Buns and Biscuits

All cooking contains something of the essential being of the cook, so how dare anyone use the word 'plain'? Perhaps 'unostentatious' would be a better word.

In this opening chapter you will find some of the simpler, less fancy cakes. But don't get the wrong idea. They must be made with as much loving care as any of the more elaborate recipes that follow. Remember the anecdote about the leading chefs being judged on their scrambled eggs? This is as good a place as any for you to show your skill.

British cookery is rich in such recipes and all of them can be superb despite memories that those of my age group may have of that bright yellow slab cake, the 'yellow terror', that was occasionally foisted on us in the forces. I spent a long time trying to decide which to include or, more accurately, which to omit. Finally I settled for a few of my favourites. I hope that your taste and mine will coincide on some of them at least.

Basic Cake Mix

Many of the comments I make here are based on the assumption that your experience in cake making and pastry cookery is limited. If you are a skilled pastry cook already, I apologise and trust that you will bear with me. This recipe in particular is for the inexperienced pastry cook and I say this not because it needs less skill, less concentration, less dedication, less

8 oz (230 g) plain flour
2 level teaspoons baking powder
6 oz (175 g) butter
6 oz (175 g) caster sugar
3 eggs
a little milk
$\frac{1}{8}$ teaspoon salt

7" (20 cm) cake tin, lined – sieve – 2 bowls – whisk – spatula

1 Sift together nearly all the flour, the salt and the baking powder.
2 Cream together the butter and sugar until it is

love than any other but because mastering it will enable you to boast of having a small repertoire of cakes at your finger tips almost immediately — and that must surely be satisfying.

OVEN TEMPERATURE:
350°F/180°C/GAS 4

white and fluffy, being careful not to over mix as the butter can easily separate.

3 Break the eggs into the creamed butter one at a time and ensure that each one is well blended in before adding the next. This process needs care and common sense. The mixing should be done steadily; should there be any sign of the eggs curdling, add a little of the flour left out of the first mix.

4 Should there be any of the 'spare flour' left, add this to the dry mix.

5 Stir the dry mix slowly and steadily into the butter and egg mix, adding just enough milk to make it a fairly soft batter. Be very sparing with the milk as the mix must not be too runny but about the texture of good double cream.

6 Put the mix into the lined cake tin evenly. I usually give the tin a little shake to make sure there are no bubbles.

7 Bake between 1 and 1½ hours until the cake is gently firm to the touch and light brown in colour.

This mix can be adapted for several other 'plain' cakes:

For SEED CAKE add two or three teaspoons of caraway seed to the dry mix.
For MADEIRA CAKE add the grated rind of at least one lemon to the dry mix and place a few pieces of candied lemon peel on top of the cake before baking.
For GINGER CAKE add at least half a teaspoon of ground ginger and 3 or 4 oz (85–115 g) of coarsely chopped, crystallised ginger to the dry mix.
For CHERRY CAKE add not less than 4 oz (115 g) glacé cherries cut in half.

The variations are many. Should you find at the first attempt that the fruit sinks to the bottom of the cake, then at the second and subsequent attempts be still more sparing with the milk.

Basic Sponges

The next few recipes together with whipped cream, jam or butter cream, and possibly some fondant, will enable you to make a vast variety of gâteaux and pastries. If you are a novice I urge you to perfect these first; so many other mixings are no more than variations on these basic themes. If you can make a really good sponge then you are more than half way to an enviable reputation as a great home baker.

OVEN TEMPERATURE:
350°F/180°C/GAS 4

4 eggs
1 oz (30 g) cornflour
1 oz (30 g) plain flour
a pinch of salt
2 oz (55 g) caster sugar
½ teaspoon vanilla

11″ × 16″ (28 cm × 40 cm) oven tray – 3 bowls – whisk – palette knife – sieve

1 Separate the yolks and the whites of the eggs into the two bowls.
2 Sift together the flour and cornflour.
3 Add the pinch of salt to the whites and beat until the mixture will just hold points.
4 Continue beating, adding the sugar a little at a time until a very firm texture is obtained. Take care not to over mix as the mixture will fall back.
5 In the other bowl, break up the yolks and add the vanilla.
6 Into the yolks fold in about a quarter of the beaten egg whites. Mix gently but thoroughly.
7 Pour the egg yolk mixture over the egg whites, sprinkle the mixed flour over this and fold in very gently.
8 Bake for 8–12 minutes until just beginning to brown.

For BASIC CHOCOLATE SPONGE SHEET proceed as for Basic Sponge Sheet, adding 1 oz (30 g) of cocoa to the flour and cornflour mix.

These sheets can be used for: Dips (see page 52) and Swiss Roll (see page 44).

Genoese

A common variation of the basic sponge and nothing to do with Genoa.

3½ oz (100 g) plain flour
4 oz (115 g) butter
6 large eggs
7 oz (200 g) caster sugar
1 teaspoon vanilla

3

OVEN TEMPERATURE:
350°F/180°C/GAS 4

3 × 7″ (20 cm) cake tins, greased or lined, or 11″ × 16″ (30 cm × 40 cm) baking tray, lined – spoon – large bowl – large saucepan – small saucepan – cup – whisk – sieve – spatula

1 Sift the flour.
2 In the small saucepan melt and clarify the butter and place somewhere warm, not hot.
3 Break the eggs into the large bowl and add the sugar. Stir until well mixed.
4 Put about 2″ (5 cm) of water into the large saucepan and bring this to simmering point. Place the large bowl over the saucepan making sure that the bottom of the bowl is well clear of the bottom of the saucepan. From time to time stir the mixture gently but thoroughly. Continue this for about ten minutes until the mixture is a brilliant yellow and lukewarm. Under no circumstances must it be allowed to start setting. Remove mixture from heat.
5 Whisk the mixture thoroughly. This can take up to half an hour by hand. The whisking should continue until the mixture is about three times its original volume and looks something like whipped cream. Clear the sides of the bowl from time to time with a spatula and take care not to over mix.
6 Fold in the flour a little at a time, and then the clarified butter and the vanilla.
7 Pour the mixture into the prepared cake tins or baking tray, ensuring that the mixture is evenly spread and that there are no bubbles.
8 Bake for about 25 minutes until mixture pulls away from the sides of the tin, is golden brown and gently firm to the touch.
9 Remove from tins to cool.

For LEMON GENOESE add one teaspoon of grated lemon peel and two tablespoons of lemon juice to the clarified butter and proceed as for Genoese.

For CHOCOLATE GENOESE replace a third to one half of the flour with cocoa powder, sift the cocoa and flour together and proceed as for Genoese.

The cakes from the cake tins can be used for: layer cakes and plain sponge cakes.

The sheet from the baking trays can be used for: Cake Strips (see page 95); Slices (see page 95); Dips (see page 52) and Swiss Rolls (see page 44).

Basic Pound Cake

Just because it is called basic *pound cake there is no reason not to treat it with respect! If you have a freezer why not make about half a dozen, or more, at a time? They keep very well in a freezer, as long as you allow them to thaw slowly when you intend to use them. You need never have mid-morning coffee or afternoon tea without something to go with it.*

OVEN TEMPERATURE: 350°F/180°C/GAS 4

6 eggs
10 oz (285 g) butter
8 oz (230 g) caster sugar
5 oz (145 g) plain flour
2 teaspoons vanilla
a pinch of salt

9″ cake tin (25 cm) – 3 bowls – tablespoon – fork – sieve – whisk

1 Separate the eggs into two of the bowls.
2 In the remaining bowl cream the softened butter with a quarter of the sugar until light and fluffy.
3 Add egg yolks one at a time, beating well after each addition and add the vanilla.
4 Add a pinch of salt to the egg whites and beat until they hold soft peaks.
5 Add the remaining sugar, a tablespoon at a time, beating well for at least 5 minutes or until the egg whites are very firm.
6 Fold a quarter of the stiffly beaten egg whites into the creamed butter mixture.
7 Pour this mixture back on top of the remaining egg whites.
8 Fold gently together, sprinkling in the sifted flour, taking care not to over mix.
9 Place the mixture into the prepared greased and floured tin.
10 Bake in the pre-set oven for about 50 minutes, until the cake is golden brown and pulls away from the sides of the tin.

Some simple variations on this basic recipe:

For NUT CAKE add 6 oz (175 g) crushed walnuts or pecans to the mixture.

For SEED CAKE add caraway seeds to the mixture.

Sussex Black Cake

I have been unbelievably lucky all my life. Time and again events that ought to have had disastrous results have turned out to further my well-being. Of course, one or two things have happened that I would prefer to forget, but if I draw up a sort of balance sheet of my life I find I am heavily in debt. High up on the long list of good things that have happened to me is that in 1974 I found a house I could afford to buy in the delightful village of Horsted Keynes in beautiful Sussex. I cannot be sure that you will like this cake. As far as I am concerned it is a Sussex cake and, as such, it is marvellous.

OVEN TEMPERATURE:
325°F/165°C/GAS 3

6 oz (180 g) butter
4 oz (130 g) caster sugar
4 oz (130 g) black treacle
3 eggs
$\frac{1}{8}$ pint (0.5 dl) milk
8 oz (230 g) assorted dried fruit
8 oz (230 g) plain flour
$\frac{1}{2}$ oz (15 g) baking powder

saucepan – bowl – sieve – spatula or strong whisk – 8″ (20 cm) cake tin, greased

1 Cream the butter and sugar together.
2 Add the black treacle and beat it well in.
3 Add the eggs one at a time.
4 Warm the milk slightly.
5 Add the milk and fruit and mix in well.
6 Sieve in the flour and baking powder and beat in well.
7 Put the mixture in the cake tin.
8 Bake in the pre-set oven for 2–2$\frac{1}{2}$ hours.

Raisin and Orange Cake

The best things in life are free – or almost. This cake, for example, is simple, unpretentious, inexpensive and delicious.

OVEN TEMPERATURE:
325°F/160°C/GAS 3

8 oz (230 g) plain flour
$\frac{1}{2}$ oz (15 g) baking powder
4 oz (115 g) margarine
4 oz (115 g) raisins
4 oz (115 g) caster sugar
2 eggs
2–3 tablespoons orange juice
grated rind of 1 orange
halved walnuts for decoration

6″ or 7″ (15 cm or 20 cm) round cake tin, greased or lined – whisk – palette knife – cooling rack – bowl

1 Place all the ingredients, except the walnuts, in the mixing bowl.
2 Beat until the mixture is well blended.
3 Pour the mixture into the prepared cake tin, making sure to level the top with the palette knife.
4 Place the tin near the bottom of the oven and bake for about $1\frac{1}{2}$ hours.
5 Remove from the oven and leave for a few minutes.
6 Turn the cake on to the cooling rack.
7 Decorate with the halved walnuts.

This cake is at its best when eaten fresh.

Chocolate Cake

Possibly the most popular of all cakes is the chocolate cake. In the world of commercial pastry cooks, some make one cake and some make another, but they all make chocolate cake of varying sizes, shapes and quality. I remember one I bought in the Midlands that looked superb and was absolutely tasteless. I often wonder how that was accomplished.

OVEN TEMPERATURE:
350°F/180°C/GAS 4

7 oz (200 g) plain flour
8 eggs
10 oz (285 g) plain chocolate
10 oz (285 g) butter
10 oz (285 g) caster sugar

thick saucepan or double boiler – 3 bowls – spatula – whisk – 9" (25 cm) cake tin, lined

1 Sift the flour.
2 Separate the eggs into two bowls.
3 Lightly beat the yolks.
4 Beat the egg whites until they are stiff and form points. A small pinch of salt may help to obtain a good consistency.
5 In the saucepan or double boiler, slowly melt the chocolate. Never subject the chocolate to an over-violent change in temperature or allow it to over-heat.
6 While the chocolate is melting, cream together the butter and sugar in the third bowl until it is quite smooth and nearly white.
7 Add the melted chocolate to the creamed butter slowly and steadily, beating the mixture all the time.
8 Add the beaten egg whites and sifted flour alternately; a little egg, a little flour, a little egg, and so on.

9 Continue to mix until the whole is thoroughly blended.

10 Put mixture into the lined cake tin, spreading evenly to avoid bubbles and making the centre a little lower than the sides.

11 Bake for about 1½ hours until the cake is well set and a good, even colour.

12 Remove from cake tin and allow to cool on a rack.

Coffee Walnut Cake

There is something about walnuts that seems to go well with coffee. There is certainly something about coffee that goes well with cake. So let's put them all together . . .

OVEN TEMPERATURE:
375°F/190°C/GAS 5

8 oz (230 g) plain flour
1 teaspoon baking powder
2 teaspoons coffee powder
4 oz (115 g) butter
4 oz (115 g) caster sugar
2 eggs
3 teaspoons warm milk
3 oz (85 g) chopped walnuts

2 × 7" or 8" (20 cm) baking tins, lined – 2 bowls – sieve – spatula

1 Sift together the flour, baking powder and coffee powder.

2 Cream together the fat and sugar until white and fluffy, taking care not to let the butter separate.

3 Break the eggs into this mixture, one at a time.

4 Fold in the flour, slowly but steadily.

5 Add the milk and mix in thoroughly.

6 Add in the chopped walnuts and stir just enough to spread them through the mix. The mixing is almost complete before the walnuts are added so take care not to over mix.

7 Divide the mix equally into the two cake tins and make sure it is evenly spread.

8 Bake for 35–40 minutes until well firm.

9 Remove from the baking tin as soon as possible and allow to cool.

Dundee Cake

The Scots are a charming and talented people and Dundee Cake is one of their most inspired creations. Unfortunately, a few commercial versions of this fine cake taste as if they had been made from sand held together with carpenter's glue. But there is another way as my friend, who teaches law at the University of Dundee, well knows . . .

OVEN TEMPERATURE:
350°F/180°C/GAS 4

12 oz (345 g) plain flour
1 level teaspoon baking powder
¼ teaspoon salt
7 oz (200 g) butter
7 oz (200 g) caster sugar
7 eggs
16 oz (460 g) mixed fruit, i.e. raisins, sultanas, chopped cherries, etc.
2 oz (60 g) malt
2½ oz (72 g) blanched almonds
a little milk

8″ (20 cm) cake tin, lined – 2 bowls – sieve – whisk – spatula

1 Toss dried fruit in a little of the flour to ensure that it does not stick together and is evenly spread through the cake.
2 Sift the flour, salt and baking powder together.
3 In the bowl, cream together the butter and caster sugar until it is light and nearly white, remembering not to over beat as this can cause the butter to separate.
4 Add the flour and eggs alternately; some of the flour, one egg, more flour, etc. Beat steadily all the time.
5 Gently stir in the fruit and the malt.
6 If the mixture begins to get hard and tacky, add a little milk very slowly. Only just enough milk to make the mix 'workable' should be added as if it becomes too soft all the fruit will sink to the bottom.
7 Put the mixture evenly into the cake tin and smooth top.
8 Place the blanched almonds on top of the cake. To make it look really nice the almonds should be put on in neat concentric circles, starting at the outside edge and working to the centre. Other, quicker methods can be used but they look like other, quicker methods!
9 Bake at the pre-set temperature for 45 minutes, then reduce the temperature to 315°F (155°C) Gas 2–3 and bake for about another 1¾ hours.

Ginger Cake

Certain things, peppermint, aniseed, almond paste, ginger and a few others have a taste to which no one is indifferent. People love or loathe them. Smoked salmon I can take or leave. I wouldn't cross the road for a glass of champagne. Aniseed is the only flavour I really dislike. But ginger – ah ginger – that is something different!

Basic Pound Cake recipe (see page 35)
3 oz (85 g) chopped, preserved ginger or candied ginger
6 oz (175 g) mixed, diced and candied fruit
1 teaspoon ground ginger
⅛ pint (0.75 dl) cooking brandy

1 Mix the preserved ginger and fruit in a bowl.
2 Add the brandy.
3 Allow to stand for 20 minutes, then drain the excess liquid.
4 Toss the fruit into a cup of flour (from the pound cake recipe).
5 Follow the pound cake recipe, adding the ginger mixture to the mix when it is otherwise complete (i.e. between stages 8 and 9 of the pound cake recipe).

Raisin Cake

Another good plain cake based on the pound cake recipe.

Basic Pound Cake recipe (see page 35).
6 oz (175 g) mixed sultanas and raisins
⅛ pint (0.75 dl) cooking brandy

1 Soak the dried fruit in the brandy for at least half an hour.
2 Drain off the excess liquid.
3 Toss the dried fruit lightly in a cup of flour (from pound cake recipe).
4 Follow the recipe for basic pound cake.
5 Fold the floured raisins and sultanas into batter with the beaten eggs.

Old-Fashioned Gingerbread

Of all the songs that the marvellously versatile Marian Montgomery sings – she is at home with jazz, blues, torch songs and even the occasional madrigal – my favourite, I think, is 'Gingerbread Man'. This recipe is for her.

10 oz (285 g) plain flour
1 teaspoon ground ginger
½ teaspoon ground cinnamon
pinch of salt
4 ozs (115 g) chopped dates
5 oz (145 g) treacle or golden syrup
3 oz (85 g) margarine
1 egg
4 oz (115 g) demerara sugar
¾ teaspoon baking powder dissolved in 3 teaspoons of milk

OVEN TEMPERATURE:
325°F/160°C/GAS 3

square tin, greased or lined – 2 bowls – saucepan – whisk – cup – knife – sieve – baking tray

1 In one bowl sieve together the flour, ground ginger, cinnamon and salt.
2 Chop and add the dates.
3 Put the treacle and margarine in the saucepan over a gentle heat, allow to melt, mix together gently and cool slowly.
4 In the other bowl beat the sugar and the egg.
5 Mix the baking powder in the cup with the milk.
6 Add the melted fat and syrup to the flour alternately with the beaten egg and sugar.
7 Add the dissolved baking powder to the mixture and mix well to a soft consistency, adding a little water if necessary.
8 Spread the mixture evenly in the prepared cake tin.
9 Bake for $1\frac{1}{2}$–2 hours.

Apple Cake

Apple cakes tend to be associated with big, informal parties. It may be because they were once very cheap to make. Alas, those days are long since past.

OVEN TEMPERATURE:
350°F/180°C/GAS 4

8 oz (230 g) flour
2 teaspoons baking powder
2 oz (60 g) butter
2 oz (60 g) lard
4 oz (115 g) granulated sugar
1 egg
8 oz (230 g) eating apples, preferably Cox's Orange Pippin or Granny Smith
$\frac{1}{4}$ pint (1.5 dl) milk
1–2 oz (30–60 g) demerara sugar

7" (20 cm) cake tin, greased – sieve – bowl – apple peeler – apple corer – sharp knife – wooden spoon

1 Sift the flour and baking powder into the bowl.
2 Mix the butter and lard together.
3 Rub the fat into the flour to achieve a crumbly texture.
4 Add the sugar and egg and mix in thoroughly.
5 Peel, core and dice the apples.

6 Stir these well into the mixture.

7 Stir in a little milk to obtain a firm consistency (will stick to spoon but can be shaken off).

8 Put mixture into cake tin and bake for about 1¾ hours but if the cake seems to be colouring too quickly or too fiercely, reduce the temperature a little.

9 Sprinkle with brown sugar while still hot.

Two simple variations are to add 2–3 oz (60–85 g) of sultanas or raisins to the mix and/or to add a little cinammon or bun spice when you dust with the sugar.

Hazelnut Cake

Almonds have an intriguing bitter-sweet flavour, walnuts have a very special tang of their own, the texture of cashews is delicious, but for me the nuttiest of all nuts is the hazelnut. Added to a cake mix they give the finished cake that very special flavour – how can I describe it? That – that – that nutty flavour!

OVEN TEMPERATURE:
375°F/190°C/GAS 5

4 oz (60 g) hazelnuts
3 oz (85 g) butter
5 oz (145 g) caster sugar
2 eggs
12 oz (345 g) plain flour
¾ oz (22 g) baking powder
¼ teaspoon salt
a little milk

7″ (20 cm) cake tin, lined – 2 bowls – coffee or nutmeg grinder – sieve – whisk

1 Grind the hazelnuts. (If you have no grinder the nuts can be bought ready ground but unless they are perfectly fresh they will have lost some of their flavour.)

2 Sift together the flour, salt and baking powder.

3 Cream the butter and sugar together until white and fluffy, taking care that the butter does not separate.

4 Add the eggs one at a time. Make sure the first egg is well blended in before adding the second.

5 Fold in the flour, adding just enough milk to keep the mixture from getting too dry. Add the milk a little at a time as you can always put in more but you can't take out the excess if you've added too much.

6 Fold in the ground hazelnuts, adding a little milk again if necessary.

7 Put the mixture into the cake tin.

8 Place the tin in the centre of a pre-heated oven for 1½ hours.

9 Reduce heat to 325°F (160°C) Gas 3 and continue to bake for another hour.

Date Loaf

The wind is howling, the rain or sleet is rattling against the windows, there is a clap of thunder. But all that is outside. Indoors there is a fire crackling in the hearth and you put down the Brontë or Dickens for just long enough to pour another cup of tea, and butter another slice of date loaf . . .

OVEN TEMPERATURE: 375°F/190°C/GAS 5

4 oz (115 g) wholemeal flour
4 oz (115 g) plain flour
2 teaspoons baking powder
2 oz (60 g) butter
6 oz (175 g) stoned dates
1 egg
2 tablespoons golden syrup
¼ pint (1.5 dl) milk

8″ (20 cm) cake tin or 1 lb (500 g) bread tin, greased – bowl – sieve – wooden spoon

1 Sift both flours and baking powder into the bowl together.

2 Rub in the butter until a crumbly texture is achieved.

3 Chop the dates (not too finely) and stir into the mixture.

4 Stir in the egg, syrup and milk and mix thoroughly but not violently.

5 Put mixture into cake tin.

6 Bake for about 1 hour.

7 Leave for a few minutes before turning out.

Other dried fruits can, of course, be used instead of dates so this is also a recipe for Cherry Loaf, Sultana Loaf, Ginger Loaf, Mixed Fruit Loaf, etc.

Tyrol Cake

If it is good and jolly the Tyroleans will do it, sing it, drink it or eat it – whichever is appropriate. This cake is, understandably, one of their favourites.

3½ oz (100 g) butter or margarine
8 oz (230 g) plain flour
1 teaspoon ground cinnamon
2 oz (60 g) caster sugar
2 oz (60 g) currants
2 oz (60 g) sultanas
¼ pint (1.5 dl) milk
1 teaspoon baking powder
3 tablespoons clear honey

OVEN TEMPERATURE:
325°F/160°C/GAS 3

6″ (15 cm) round cake tin, greased – 2 bowls – spatula – cooling rack

1 Put the butter or margarine, flour and cinnamon into one of the bowls and rub together with the tips of the fingers until you have a fine breadcrumb texture.
2 Add the washed fruit and sugar to the mixture and stir thoroughly, then make a well in the centre.
3 Dissolve the baking powder in the milk, add the clear honey and pour this into the well of the mixture.
4 Gradually work in the dry ingredients, adding a little more milk if necessary, just sufficient to give the mixture a dropping consistency.
5 Pour the mixture into the prepared cake tin and bake in the pre-set oven for 1¾–2 hours or until the cake is well risen and firm to touch.
6 Remove from the oven and turn out on to cooling rack.

Swiss Roll

Some people make the most superb, light, almost frothy, Swiss Rolls. Others, using the same recipe and method, produce something with the consistency of sponge rubber. There must be a reason for this but I don't know what it is. So, if at first you don't succeed, try, try, try again. But if you still don't succeed, give up and make something else!

OVEN TEMPERATURE:
430°F/220°C/GAS 7-8

SPONGE
3 large eggs
4 oz (115 g) caster sugar
3 oz (85 g) plain flour
1 tablespoon hot water
FILLING
3–4 oz (85–115 g) warm jam or curd
  or 2–3 oz (60–85 g) whipped cream
a little caster sugar for decoration

9″ × 12″ (25 × 30 cm) baking tray, lined – bowl – sieve – wooden spoon – palette knife – whisk – sheet of paper or cloth

1 Whisk the eggs and sugar together in the bowl.
2 Sift the flour into the mixture, folding it gently until completely even and creamy.
3 Pour mixture into lined baking tray, spreading it evenly with the palette knife, ensuring that every corner is properly filled.

4 Bake for 7–10 minutes, until firm but not dried out. (Test with finger pressure – when no dent is left cooking is complete.)

5 Turn this sponge sheet on to a sheet of paper or a cloth.

6 Spread sponge with jam or cream filling (allow it to cool first if cream filling is to be used).

7 Turn over a little of one of the long edges and roll up the remainder by pulling on the paper or cloth.

8 Sprinkle with caster sugar.

Lardy Cake

As British as the Yeomen of the Guard, as solid and reliable too.

OVEN TEMPERATURE:
400°F/205°C/GAS 6

BREAD DOUGH

½ oz (15 g) fresh yeast

½ pint (3 dl) tepid water

1 teaspoon caster sugar

1 lb (460 g) plain flour

½ teaspoon salt

FILLING

4 oz (115 g) lard

4 oz (115 g) caster sugar

4 oz (115 g) currants

a little spice

GLAZE

2 tablespoons sugar mixed with 2 tablespoons water

12″ × 7″ (30 cm × 18 cm) tin or baking sheet – 2 bowls – rolling pin – sieve – palette knife – tea towel – pastry brush

1 In one bowl cream the yeast with the sugar and add the tepid water and a little flour.

2 Put the dough in a warm place until it is covered with bubbles.

3 Add the sieved flour and salt to the dough.

4 Knead thoroughly, then cover with a tea towel and allow the dough to prove (i.e. to rise to double its original size). This will probably take about 1–1½ hours.

5 Knead again, until smooth, then roll the dough out on to a floured board to a neat oblong shape.

6 Spread half the lard, in small pieces, over two thirds of the dough.

7 Sprinkle the same area with half the sugar, fruit and spices, then fold in three bringing the uncovered piece of dough over.

8 Give this mixture half a turn, spreading the remaining lard, in small pieces, over two thirds of the surface of the dough.

9 Sprinkle the same area with the remainder of the sugar, fruit and spice and fold in three, once again bringing the uncovered pieces of dough over first.

10 Turn again and roll to a neat oblong; fold, turn and re-roll.

11 Fold the dough once more and roll out to fit the prepared warmed tin.

12 Score the top with the palette knife.

13 Cover again with the tea towel and allow 30–40 minutes to prove until well risen.

14 Bake in the centre of the oven until a golden brown.

15 Remove from the tin. To test if the cake is ready knock the base and the cake should sound hollow.

16 Glaze at once by blending the water and sugar and brush this syrup over the cake.

This mixture should make fourteen slices.

Rock Buns

Crisp and brown outside, pale and crumbly inside; rock buns should be so fresh that they still have the smell of the oven about them.

OVEN TEMPERATURE:
425°F/220°C/GAS 7

8 oz (230 g) plain flour
½ oz (15 g) baking powder
4 oz (115 g) lard
4 oz (115 g) caster sugar
4 oz (115 g) dried fruit
1 egg
a little milk to mix
a little caster sugar

2 baking trays, greased – 2 bowls – sieve – whisk – spatula – cooling rack

1 Sift the flour and baking powder into one of the bowls.

2 Rub in the lard until a very fine texture is obtained, then add the sugar and fruit.

3 In the second bowl beat the egg and add this to the mixture, using just enough milk to make a sticky consistency.

4 Drop the mixture in small heaps on to the prepared trays, making sure to leave sufficient room to allow the buns to spread during cooking.

5 Sprinkle a little sugar on to each heap and bake near the top of the oven for 12–15 minutes or until the buns are crisp and golden brown in colour.

6 Remove from the oven and place on the cooling rack.

7 Dust with a little caster sugar.

Sponge Fingers

There is nothing to stop you using four times the quantities and making four times the number of sponge fingers than I suggest here. Particularly in summer they are useful to eat with trifles and ice creams. But they are good too on their own and a favourite with babies and small children who can't seem to have enough of them.

OVEN TEMPERATURE:
400°F/205°C/GAS 6

2 eggs
2 oz (60 g) caster sugar
2 oz (60 g) plain flour
2 oz (60 g) plain chocolate

baking tray, greased and dusted with flour – 2 bowls – whisk – savoy bag with plain tube – wooden spoon – sieve – cooling tray

1 In one of the bowls put the eggs and sugar and whisk together over hot water until firm and thick.

2 Remove the bowl from the hot water.

3 Fold in the sifted flour and mix thoroughly but gently.

4 Put the mixture into the savoy bag.

5 Pipe 4″ (10 cm) 'fingers' onto the greased and floured tray.

6 Bake at the top of the oven for about 10 minutes or until the fingers are a golden colour.

7 Remove the fingers from the tray and place on a cooling tray.

8 In the second bowl, melt the chocolate over hot water.

9 Dip each end of the sponge fingers in the chocolate and allow to harden.

Madeleines

These remind me both of Paris and of tea at a little roadside café in Devon. Both memories are full of sunshine. For me, to this day, it never rains in Paris nor when I'm eating a Madeleine. I wonder who the girl was that this lovely little pastry was named after . . .

OVEN TEMPERATURE:
350°F/175°C/GAS 4

2 eggs
4 oz (115 g) butter or margarine
4 oz (115 g) caster sugar
4 oz (115 g) plain flour
red jam
desiccated coconut
glacé cherries
angelica

12 dariole moulds, greased – 2 bowls – saucepan – whisk – tablespoon – pastry brush – skewer

1 In one of the bowls beat the eggs well.
2 In the second bowl, cream the butter or margarine and the sugar until pale and fluffy.
3 Add the beaten eggs, a little at a time, beating each time.
4 Fold in half of the flour, using the tablespoon, and mix well but lightly before folding in the remainder of the flour.
5 Place the mixture into the moulds about three quarters full.
6 Bake at the top of the pre-set oven for 20 minutes.
7 Gently melt the jam in the saucepan.
8 When the cakes are cold, trim the bottoms so that they stand firmly.
9 Hold the cakes on a skewer and brush with the melted jam.
10 Roll each one in the desiccated coconut and decorate with a cherry and angelica.

Butterfly Cakes

It happens to all of us at one time or another – all the in-laws or maybe all your grown-up children's friends and would-be relatives descend on the house at once. As you look round your crowded living room you wonder how everyone managed to arrive at once and it's

CAKE
2 eggs
4 oz (115 g) margarine
4 oz (115 g) caster sugar
6 oz (175 g) plain flour
¼ oz (8 g) baking powder
FILLING
4 oz (115 g) butter
6 oz (175 g) icing sugar
almond essence

obvious that none of them has eaten for a week! How lucky you had ample warning (twenty-four hours) that they were coming and time to make a couple of mixings of butterfly cakes. . . Pity there isn't one left for you!

OVEN TEMPERATURE:
375°F/180°C/GAS 5

patty tin or paper cases for 12–15 cakes – 3 bowls – whisk – sieve – wooden spoon – piping bag – knife – teaspoon

CAKE
1 In one of the bowls beat the eggs well.
2 In the second bowl cream the margarine and sugar together until light and fluffy.
3 Add the beaten eggs a little at a time and stir well after each addition.
4 Fold in the sifted flour (with baking powder) to give a stiff dropping consistency. (A little milk may be added if necessary.)
5 Place in spoonfuls in the patty tin or paper cases.
6 Bake in the top of the oven for 15–20 minutes.
7 Allow the cakes to cool.

FILLING
1 In the third bowl, cream the butter until it is soft.
2 Beat in the sifted icing sugar gradually.
3 Add a few drops of almond essence.
4 To finish the cakes, cut a slice from the top of each and pipe on a generous amount of the filling.
5 Cut each slice that has been removed from the cakes in half and replace at an angle in the cream to form the butterfly's wings.

The filling and the cake mixture may be flavoured in various ways, for instance with grated orange or lemon and a little of the juice.

Sherry Biscuits

A country parson I knew in my youth used to invite a lot of us youngsters to tea on Saturdays. Tea on the vicarage lawn, if it was fine, in the enormous living room if it wasn't. He was a marvellous man, that parson, and he had a lovely daughter and a wife who made the most superb, melt-in-your mouth

1 egg
5 oz (145 g) plain flour
4 oz (115 g) butter
3 oz (85 g) caster sugar
1 tablespoon sherry, medium
2–3 oz (60–85 g) chopped almonds

sieve – bowl – 2 cups or small bowls – whisk – rolling pin – sharp pointed knife or 2" (5 cm) pastry cutter – pastry brush – 2 baking sheets, well greased

sherry biscuits. The daughter preferred some six-foot-four rugby forward who, having taken a first class honours degree in economics, had just joined a merchant bank of which his father was chairman. I was left with the sherry biscuits!

OVEN TEMPERATURE:
350°F/180°C/GAS 4

1 Separate the egg into 2 cups.
2 Sift the flour into the bowl.
3 Rub in the butter.
4 Add the sugar, egg yolk and sherry, in that order, mixing thoroughly all the while.
5 Roll the paste out about $\frac{1}{8}$″ (0.75 cm) thick.
6 Cut into fancy shapes about 2″ (5 cm) across.
7 Lightly beat the egg white.
8 Brush the biscuits with the egg white.
9 Sprinkle liberally with the chopped almonds.
10 Place on baking sheets.
11 Bake for 15–20 minutes.

Coffee Kisses

They have been known to lead to real ones!

OVEN TEMPERATURE:
350°F/180°C/GAS 4

6 oz (175 g) plain flour
1 oz (15 g) baking powder
3 oz (85 g) margarine or butter
2 oz (60 g) caster sugar
1 egg yolk
1 teaspoon coffee powder dissolved in a very little water
a little icing sugar

baking sheet, greased – bowl – spatula

1 Sift the flour and baking powder together into the bowl.
2 Rub the fat into the flour and add the sugar.
3 Add the egg yolk and coffee to the mixture until it forms a stiff paste, bind well by hand.
4 Roll the mixture into balls the size of a small walnut.
5 Place these on the greased baking sheet, leaving sufficient space between each one.
6 Bake in oven for about 15 minutes.
7 Allow to cool and put together with coffee butter cream (see page 128).
8 Dust with icing sugar.

Meringues

Meringues are enormously popular. I know because of the huge number of them that we sell. Our customers tell me that our meringues are very good, and who am I to argue with them? I don't happen to like meringues myself. I hope you do.

OVEN TEMPERATURE:
200°F maximum/95°C/GAS below ¼

5 egg whites
¼ teaspoon cream of tartar
¼ teaspoon salt
1 teaspoon vanilla
9 oz (255 g) caster sugar

2 × 11″ × 16″ (30 cm × 40 cm) baking trays – bowl – whisk – piping bag and tubes

1 Mix together the egg whites, cream of tartar, salt and vanilla.
2 Whisk together until the mixture will make small points.
3 Add about half the sugar and continue to beat until mixture is very stiff. Test for complete mixing by rubbing a little of the mixture between thumb and finger; if sugar grain can no longer be felt mixing is complete.
4 Fold in remainder of the sugar.
5 Grease and flour the baking tray. Desired shapes may be marked onto the flour on the tray as a guide.
6 Pipe mixture on to tray using the right size of tube for the effect that you want.
7 Place baking sheet in oven. Leave at about 200°F (95°C) Gas below ¼ for some 15 minutes then turn off the heat and leave for at least five hours or, better still, overnight. Too fast baking will result in loss of colour, texture and flavour as well as the cook's reputation!

Meringues may be served by piping whipped cream on to the flat side of one meringue and making a sandwich of it with another. This confection can be decorated with a glacé cherry or a piece of angelica. Another way to serve meringues is with their flat sides dipped in molten chocolate.

By the way, I have been told of many short cuts for making meringues but I haven't yet found one that's satisfactory. If you need meringues in a hurry, buy them!

Fondant Dips

A simple, attractive and popular dish to offer at all tea parties, but particularly to children. Make lots of them in lots of different colours.

1 sheet sponge or Genoese, plain or chocolate, (see pages 33–4)
8 oz (230 g) jam
12 oz (345 g) butter-cream, flavoured to taste (see page 128)
1 pint (5.5 dl) whipped cream (see page 127)

or any permutations of these

1 lb (460 g) fondant, coloured (see page 130)
walnuts, glacé cherries, angelica, chocolate drops or other decoration

sharp knife – palette knife – saucepan – wire rack – metal tray

1 Cut the sponge or Genoese in two horizontally.
2 Spread the jam, cream or butter-cream over the lower part and replace the top.
3 Cut the filled sheet into strips about 2″ (5 cm) wide and then cut these strips into slices about 1″ (2.5 cm) wide.
4 Place as many of these as will fit on to the wire rack which is standing on the metal tray. Leave sufficient space between the portions of sponge (Genoese) to allow the fondant to pour down the sides.
5 Melt and colour the fondant gently and pour it over the portions. (Keep the fondant over a gentle heat.)
6 After pouring the first time the spilt fondant on the tray under the rack should be scraped up with the palette knife and mixed with the fondant still in the saucepan to re-melt.
7 Decorate as desired.

Chelsea Buns

What an odd assortment of things are associated with Chelsea – army pensioners, flower shows, artists and buns!

BUN DOUGH
1 oz (30 g) sugar
½ oz (15 g) fresh yeast
¼ pint (1.5 dl) warm milk
8 oz (230 g) plain flour
a pinch of salt

OVEN TEMPERATURE:
450°F/230°C/GAS 8

FILLING
1 oz (30 g) butter or margarine
1 oz (30 g) sugar
2 oz (60 g) dried fruit

GLAZE
1 tablespoon hot water
1 tablespoon sugar

11″ × 16″ (30 cm × 40 cm) baking tray – small saucepan – 2 bowls – sieve – rolling pin – pastry brush – knife – teaspoon – tablespoon – tea towel

BUN DOUGH
1 Warm the milk in the saucepan, add the sugar and dissolve and stir in the yeast.
2 In one bowl sieve the flour and salt and add the remaining sugar and the yeast liquid.
3 Cover the dough with a tea towel and allow to rise (for about 50 minutes at room temperature) until the dough is double its original size.
4 Knead the dough until it is smooth and roll out to a neat oblong.

FILLING
1 Spread the rolled out dough with the softened butter, sprinkle with sugar and dried fruit.
2 Roll the dough up like a swiss roll and cut into portions about ½″ (1½ cm) thick, placing on the warm tray.
3 Cover the dough again with the tea towel to rise for a further 20 minutes.
4 Bake in a pre-set oven for 10–15 minutes.
5 To glaze, blend the water and sugar and brush over the buns.

Sally Lunns

In every county in England I have visited – and there are not many I haven't – somebody has claimed that the Sally Lunn originated there. But what does it matter where they come from? It wouldn't

1 oz (30 g) lard or other fat
¼ pint (1.5 dl) milk
½ oz (15 g) yeast
12 oz (345 g) plain flour
2 oz (60 g) caster sugar
1 egg
a good pinch of salt
glaze (a little melted fat)

surprise me to hear that the Americans and Chinese claim them too. The important thing is they're here now.

OVEN TEMPERATURE: 375°F/190°C/GAS 5

4 small cake tins – 3 bowls – saucepan – whisk – pastry brush – teaspoon

1 Melt the fat in the saucepan, add the milk and warm to blood heat.
2 In one bowl cream the yeast with a teaspoon of sugar.
3 Mix in the yeast with the fat and the milk.
4 In the second bowl, mix the flour, salt and sugar and add this to the yeast liquid.
5 In the third bowl, beat the egg well then add the yeast liquid to the beaten egg and beat until a light dough is obtained.
6 Divide the dough into four pieces and knead each piece well.
7 Put the dough into the greased and floured cake tins, pricking the tops lightly and leave to rise to the tops of the tins.
8 Bake for 20 minutes until they are firm to the touch.
9 Remove from the tins and brush the tops with a little of the melted fat.

Just a Little Bit More Exciting

These recipes are neither 'better' nor even 'more difficult' than the earlier ones, but they are, perhaps, a little less frequently made at home. Don't be afraid to try them.

Savarin Dough Cakes

In Hungary, near the Austrian border, there is a town called Szombathely (Saturday place). The Romans, for reasons of their own, called it Savaria. I would like to be able to say that that is where this excellent dough originated – it did not!

OVEN TEMPERATURE:
400°F/205°C/GAS 6

½ oz (15 g) yeast
1½ oz (45 g) caster sugar
½ teaspoon salt
½ cupful lukewarm milk
4 eggs
up to 8 oz (230 g) plain flour
5 oz (140 g) slightly softened butter

large bowl – 9″ (25 cm) savarin ring or 24 small baba rings, greased, and a baking tray on which to put them – whisk

1 Cream together yeast, sugar and salt.
2 Stir in the milk and the lightly beaten eggs and add enough flour to make a soft, batter-like mixture.
3 Beat this thoroughly until it is completely blended, taking care not to whip it.
4 Cover the bowl and leave it to stand somewhere warm, but not hot, for about 45 minutes, until the mixture has doubled in volume.
5 Knock the mixture back (see page 147).
6 Add the softened butter which should not be liquid.
7 Put the mixture into the savarin ring or the baba moulds, half filling them.
8 Leave them to stand until the mixture doubles in volume to fill the moulds.
9 Place in pre-heated oven, 400°F (205°C) Gas 6 for the first 10 minutes for the large savarin and five minutes for the small babas.

10 Reduce the heat to 350°F (180°C) Gas 4 and continue to bake until cakes are firm and a rich golden colour, about 10–15 minutes for the babas and up to 40 minutes for the ring.

Cheesecake

This is one of the most delicious dishes from the Jewish cuisine and as far as I can gather almost every Jewish housewife has the one and only recipe for this confection. How then do I dare to include a recipe here? It seems that quite a few cookery book writers have stopped short at this challenge so the mere fact that I am plunging ahead should put this book into a certain select class! I cannot claim that this recipe is 'the best'. That remains a subjective judgement. It is, however, a recipe that I like.

OVEN TEMPERATURE:
300°F/150°C/GAS 1–2

3 eggs
14 oz (415 g) cream cheese
4 oz (115 g) caster sugar
⅛ pint (1.5 dl) whipping cream
1 oz (30 g) cornflour
1 oz (30 g) plain flour
1 thin, round 8″ (20 cm) sponge (see page 33)
a little jam

2 bowls – whisk – spatula – 8″ (20 cm) flan tin, greased

1 Separate the eggs into the two bowls.
2 To the yolks add the cheese, sugar and cream and mix well.
3 Add the flour slowly and mix until completely smooth and creamy.
4 Whip the egg whites until they are stiff.
5 Fold in the cornflour carefully and thoroughly.
6 Blend the yolk-cheese mix into the egg white mix.
7 Spread the jam on one side of the sponge.
8 Place the sponge – jam side up – in the flan tin.
9 Pour the mixture into the flan tin.
10 Bake for about 1½ hours.

Almond Butter Cake

Although the finished article may not look spectacular there is something about it that, to me at any rate, spells luxuriant leisure. I somehow can't imagine having a piece of almond butter cake – plain or chocolate – with a hastily

2½ oz (70 g) clarified butter
3 whole eggs and a further 2 egg yolks
2 oz (55 g) almond paste
½ teaspoon vanilla
3½ oz (100 g) caster sugar
1 teaspoon grated lemon rind
3 oz (85 g) plain flour

11″ × 16″ (30 cm × 40 cm) baking tray or 9″ (25 cm) cake tin – 2 bowls – large saucepan – small saucepan – whisk – sieve

grabbed cup of tea in that two minute break between digging the vegetable garden and clearing a blocked sink. Come to think of it, there's no good reason for not using this mixture for a gâteau, so come on, get inventing!

OVEN TEMPERATURE:
350°F/180°C/GAS 4

1 Clarify the butter in small saucepan.
2 In one bowl gently but very thoroughly mix together the almond paste and an egg yolk until a smooth light texture is obtained.
3 In the other bowl mix together the whole eggs, the remaining egg yolk, the vanilla, sugar and grated lemon rind.
4 Put about 2″ (5 cm) of water into the large saucepan and bring to simmering point. Place the large bowl over the saucepan so that the bowl is clear of the water. Stir the mixture gently but thoroughly from time to time. Continue this for about 10 minutes until the mixture is a brilliant yellow and lukewarm. Remove mixture from heat.
5 Pour on and fold in the almond paste and then the flour, taking great care not to over mix.
6 Spread the mixture evenly in the cake tin or baking tray making sure there are no 'wrinkles' or bubbles.
7 Bake for about 20 minutes.

For CHOCOLATE ALMOND BUTTER CAKE replace one third to one half of the flour with cocoa powder. Sift the cocoa and flour together and proceed as for Almond Butter Cake.

These sheets can be used for: Dips (see page 52), Swiss Rolls (see page 44) and Yule Logs (see page 108).

Cream Horns

Traditionally, the horn represents the horn of plenty. I have seen cream horns filled with all sorts of things other than whipped cream. There is no law against that but I wish there was one. It is a 'fun thing' but, in its unfussy way the cream horn manages to have a sort of dignity.

flaky or puff pastry (see pages 134–5)
a little water
caster sugar for coating horns
granulated sugar for whipping into cream
whipping cream

pastry board – sharp knife – rolling pin – whisk – horn moulds, greased – savoy bag with large pipe – baking sheet, greased

1 Roll out the pastry fairly thinly so that one edge is about 10″–12″ (25–30 cm) long.

OVEN TEMPERATURE:
450°F/232°C/GAS 8

2 Cut it into strips ½″ (1.25 cm) wide and 10″–12 (25–30 cm) long.
3 Starting at the pointed end 'bandage' the horn mould so that every layer half overlaps the preceding one.
4 Brush with water.
5 Sprinkle with, or dip into, caster sugar.
6 Place on baking sheet and bake for 10–15 minutes.
7 Whip the cream with the granulated sugar.
8 Fill savoy bag and pipe into the horns when these are cold.
9 If you want to add a party touch, decorate with a strawberry.

Cream Slices

Make the pastry with extra care, making sure that it is really crisp – if in doubt leave it in the oven a moment or two longer. Leave putting the cream on the pastry as late as conveniently possible. The result should be a cream slice you can be truly proud of. Be slapdash about the whole business and you'll come up with a couple of layers of wet blotting paper with a mixture of axle grease and whitewash between them. And, by the way, why not try filling the slice with pastry cream (see page 129) instead of whipped cream! For my taste that is even better.

OVEN TEMPERATURE:
475°F/245°C/GAS 9

flaky or puff pastry (see pages 134–5)
1 pint (5.5 dl) whipping cream
a pinch of salt
3 oz (85 g) caster sugar
4 oz (115 g) strained jam
2 oz (60 g) icing sugar or fondant mixture

bowl – whisk – pastry board – rolling pin – sharp knife – baking sheet, greased – palette knife – sieve

1 Roll out the fresh pastry to about ¼″ (0.5 cm) thick.
2 Place on greased baking sheet, trimming the edges if necessary.
3 Bake for 20–25 minutes.
4 While pastry is baking, whip the cream, adding the pinch of salt first and the sugar gradually.
5 When pastry is baked, remove from baking sheet and cut it in half horizontally.
6 Cut one half of the sheet into pieces the size of cream slice required, usually about 3″ × 1½″ (8 cm × 4 cm).
7 Spread the strained jam (i.e. jam warmed to liquid and seived to remove skin and pips) evenly on the uncut half.
8 Cover the jam with whipped cream.
9 Place the pieces of cut pastry on top of the cream.

10 Cut through the creamed layer using the cut pieces as guides.

11 Place dusting sugar in sieve or dusting bag and dust over.

Instead of dusting sugar, fondant may be used. In this case allow about 4 oz (115 g) of fondant (see page 130), a teaspoon of instant coffee and proceed thus:

1 Before cutting the half sheet into individual pieces, soften the fondant in a double boiler.

2 Spread about three quarters of it evenly over the half pastry sheet.

3 Flavour and colour the remaining fondant by mixing the instant coffee into it while still warm.

4 Put flavoured fondant into forcing bag with fine pipe and draw several parallel lines over the white fondant.

5 Draw a knife lightly across this at right angles to fondant lines and in alternate directions to give marbled effect.

Ischler Biscuits

At the end of this recipe I have written:'These biscuits will keep for several days.' That is, if you put them under lock and key!

OVEN TEMPERATURE:
325°F/160°C/GAS 3

5 oz (145 g) butter
3½ oz (100 g) plain flour
3 oz (85 g) grated almonds, walnuts or hazelnuts
2¾ oz (80 g) caster sugar
a pinch of cinnamon
a little vanilla
a little raspberry or redcurrant jam for filling
8–10 oz (230–290 g) chocolate for decoration

baking sheet, greased – pastry board – rolling pin – pastry cutter 2½–3" (6–8 cm) – spatula – 2 bowls – cooling rack

1 Put the butter, sifted flour, grated almonds, walnuts or hazelnuts together with the sugar, a pinch of cinnamon and a little vanilla into one of the bowls. With the tips of the fingers mix well together until you have a smooth dough.

2 Leave the dough for an hour.

3 Put the dough on to the floured pastry board and roll it out to not less than ¼" (1·5 cm) thick.

4 Cut into biscuit-like shapes with the cutter and place on the baking sheet or tray.

5 Bake in the pre-set oven for 10–15 minutes or until they are firm and crisp.

6 Remove the biscuits from the oven and put them on the cooling rack.

7 When cool paste the biscuits together in pairs with the raspberry or redcurrant jam.

8 Melt the chocolate carefully and pour it over the biscuits, then let them dry.

These biscuits will keep for several days.

Rigo Jancsi

The Gypsies are a proud and splendid people. Perhaps none more so than the Hungarian gypsies who are famous throughout the world for their musical skill. One of the greatest of all gypsy violinists was Rigo Jancsi (Johnny Blackbird), who is said to have loved good food as much as he loved good music. Jancsi played his magical violin in all the best restaurants in Budapest and wherever he played the crowds followed. A grateful restaurateur created this glorious, diet-defeating confection for him.

OVEN TEMPERATURE:
360°F/180°C/GAS 4–5

CAKE

5 eggs

2½ oz (70 g) caster sugar

1½ oz (45 g) plain flour

2 small teaspoons cocoa powder

a little rum

FILLING

½ pint (3 dl) fresh whipping cream

a little chocolate

2 baking tins, preferably square, about 6" (15 cm) sq – 3 bowls – whisk – spatula – palette knife – cooling rack – saucepan

CAKE

1 Separate the egg yolks and whites into two of the bowls.

2 Whisk the egg whites well until they are stiff and fluffy.

3 Gradually add the egg yolks and sugar to the beaten egg whites. Continue to stir and add the flour and cocoa. Mix all the ingredients together well and add a few drops of rum.

4 Pour the mixture into the two prepared cake tins and bake in the pre-set oven until a golden brown colour.

5 Remove from the oven and turn out on to the cooling rack.

6 When cold cut each cake through the middle horizontally.

FILLING

1 Using fresh cream, whisk well until it is quite thick.

2 Melt the chocolate in the saucepan and add about half of it to the whipped cream, taking care not to add too much as this would over thicken it.

3 Spread the cream thickly and evenly between the layers of the cake.

4 To decorate, cover the cake with the remainder of the melted chocolate and leave it to cool and set.

Piskota

I mustn't start on about these or I'll never stop. They are my favourite of favourites. Multiply the quantities by ten, invite me to tea, and you won't have one piskota left by the time I leave!

OVEN TEMPERATURE:
300°F/150°C/GAS 1–2

1 lb 4 oz (590 g) caster sugar
about ¼ pint (1·5 dl) water
2 oz (60 g) instant coffee or chocolate powder dissolved in water
3 egg whites
7 oz (210 g) plain flour

bowl – large heavy saucepan, minimum 2 pint (6 dl) – baking tray, greased – piping bag with medium size plain tube – sugar thermometer

1 Put the sugar and coffee solution into the saucepan, mix well together and bring up to a temperature of 280°F (140°C), stirring occasionally.

2 While the sugar mixture is boiling, whip the egg whites in the bowl until they are really stiff.

3 Add the boiled sugar mixture to the egg whites and continue whisking.

4 Stir in the flour gently and continue to stir very gently until the whole is well mixed together.

5 Put the mixture into the piping bag and pipe into the prepared baking tray in either 3″ (8 cm) fingers or 1″ (2·5 cm) discs.

6 These may be decorated with half walnuts or some similar addition but I feel this to be unnecessary and have not, therefore, included these among the ingredients.

7 Put the tray in a warm place (airing cupboard?) for about 15–20 minutes until the piskota form a thick, dry crust.

8 Bake in the oven for a further 15–20 minutes.

Piskota will keep perfectly well for several days if you put them in a tin and then put the tin where nobody can find it!

Rum Baba

These may look like miniature motor tyres dipped in axle grease but shouldn't taste like them!

OVEN TEMPERATURE:
425°F/220°C/GAS 7

DOUGH
$\frac{1}{8}$ pint (0.75 dl) warm milk
$\frac{2}{3}$ oz (20 g) yeast
1 lb 14 oz (860 g) plain flour
7 eggs
2 oz (60 g) butter
1 heaped tablespoon caster sugar
2 oz (60 g) sultanas or currants
a little salt
SYRUP
$\frac{1}{4}$ pint (1.5 dl) rum or kirsch
8 oz (230 g) caster sugar
$1\frac{1}{2}$ cups water
a little melted jam
fresh whipped cream

bowl, preferably wooden – sieve – 2 saucepans – tea towel – cooking thermometer – cooling rack – moulds (these may be individual or one large one, greased) – pastry brush – wooden spoon – tablespoon

DOUGH
1 Warm the milk in a saucepan and add the yeast. Allow to dissolve.

2 Sieve the flour into the bowl, making a well in the centre.

3 Put the yeast and milk into the well.

4 Add the beaten egg a little at a time, working

the dough with the hands to mix well, making sure not to leave any unmixed dough around the sides of the bowl.

5 Cut the butter into small pieces and scatter over the dough, then cover the bowl with the tea towel and put in a warm place until it has doubled in size (about 30 minutes).

6 Add the sugar and salt and knead the dough until the softened butter has been absorbed into the mixture.

7 If using the sultanas or currants, add and mix well.

8 Fill the prepared moulds to within one third of the top.

9 Bake until a golden brown (about 20–25 minutes) then remove from the oven and allow to cool before turning out.

SYRUP

1 Put the rum or kirsch, sugar and water into a saucepan and bring to the boil, 220°F (105°C), testing with the thermometer, and stir until it thickens.

2 Soak the cooked babas in the syrup for at least 5–6 minutes and place them on the cooling rack to drain.

3 Brush the babas with a little melted jam and decorate with the fresh whipped cream.

Gugelhupf

For years now we have been hearing about the German economic miracle, but this is unfair to the Germans. There are other German miracles besides – and this is one one of them.

OVEN TEMPERATURE:
350°F/180°C/GAS 4

4 eggs
4½ oz (130 g) soft butter
4½ oz (130 g) caster sugar
4½ oz (130 g) plain flour
grated rind of one lemon
a little icing sugar

fluted tin or mould, greased and floured – 3 bowls – grater – spatula – whisk – sieve – cooling rack

1 Separate the egg whites and yolks into two of the bowls.

2 In the third bowl cream the softened butter, sugar and finely grated lemon rind.

3 Beat the egg yolks and add to the cream mixture.

4 Add the sieved flour and gradually stir this into the mixture.

5 Whisk the egg whites until they are stiff and fold into the mixture lightly but evenly.

6 Put the mixture in the prepared cake tin or mould three-quarters full.

7 Bake in the pre-set oven for 30–40 minutes or until golden brown and firm to touch.

8 Turn out gently on to the cooling rack.

9 Dust with sieved icing sugar before serving.

Polish Honey Cake

The history of Poland is not a happy one. Over the centuries the Polish people have had little cause for rejoicing but, or so a Pole once told me, the bees in that country are the happiest and most industrious in the world. That, this Pole assured me, is why Polish honey is the best that there is. Whatever the truth of this Polish honey cake remains one of the world's great delicacies. What does anything matter so long as they keep on making it!

OVEN TEMPERATURE: 350°F/175°C/GAS 4

3 egg yolks
5 egg whites
4 oz (115 g) caster sugar
3 oz (85 g) chopped walnuts
8 oz (230 g) plain flour
$\frac{1}{2}$ oz (15 g) baking powder
$\frac{1}{2}$ teaspoon grated nutmeg
1 teaspoon ground cinnamon
$\frac{1}{4}$ teaspoon powdered cloves
$\frac{1}{2}$ pint (3 dl) clear honey
a little icing sugar for decoration, optional

8″ (20 cm) cake tin, greased – 2 bowls – whisk – sieve – spatula – sheet of greaseproof paper – cooling rack

1 Separate the egg whites and yolks into two bowls.

2 Add the sugar to the egg yolks and cream together until a light mixture is obtained.

3 Add the flour, baking powder, walnuts, spices and honey.

4 Beat the egg whites until stiff and firm.

5 Fold the egg whites into the mixture.

6 Put the mixture into the prepared cake tin, spreading evenly.

7 Bake in the centre of the pre-set oven for about 1 hour. If the cake shows signs of over browning, cover the top with greaseproof

Date Loaf *page 43*   Apple Cake *page 41*

Fudge Cake *page 67*

Dundee Cake *page 39*

Cream Horns *page 57*

Brandy Snaps *page 68*   Meringues *page 51*

Eclairs and Choux Buns *page 136*

paper for the remainder of the cooking time.

8 Remove from the oven and turn out on to the cooling rack.

9 This cake may be left plain or decorated with icing sugar sifted through a paper doily.

Easter Biscuits

Why Easter *biscuits! I can't imagine. It seems that our puritan tradition makes us look for excuses to have something just a little bit special. Easter never falls in August but I've eaten these biscuits then and they were very nice indeed.*

OVEN TEMPERATURE:
400°F/205°C/GAS 6

1 egg
3 oz (85 g) butter or margarine
2½ oz (70 g) caster sugar
6 oz (175 g) plain flour
¼ oz (8 g) baking powder
1½ oz (45 g) currants
½ oz (15 g) chopped mixed peel
a pinch of salt
1–2 tablespoons of milk and/or brandy
a little extra caster sugar

2 baking sheets, greased – 3 bowls – sieve – sharp knife – spatula – pastry board – rolling pin – 2½" (6 cm) fluted cutter – pastry brush – cooling rack

1 Separate the egg yolk and white.

2 Put the butter and sugar into the bowl and cream together until light and fluffy, taking care not to over beat.

3 Add the egg yolk to the butter and sugar mixture and mix well. Put the egg white aside for later.

4 Fold the sifted flour, baking powder and salt into the creamed mixture very carefully.

5 Add the currants and then the chopped mixed peel and stir all the ingredients together thoroughly but very gently.

6 Add just sufficient milk – or brandy, if you prefer – to give a fairly soft dough, then cover the dough with a cloth and leave in a cool place to become firm.

7 Put the dough on to the floured pastry board and knead lightly, then roll out to about ¼" (1.5 cm) thick, and cut the rolled out dough into rounds with the cutter.

8 Put the cut rounds on to the prepared baking sheet, spacing them well apart and bake in the pre-set oven for 10 minutes. Take them out of the oven and brush each one with a little of the egg white, then sprinkle them with sugar. Return the rounds to the oven and bake for a further 10 minutes or until they are a golden brown colour.

Honey Almond Dessert Cake

When children have been very good they deserve something special. That goes for children of all ages . . .

OVEN TEMPERATURE:
350°F/180°C/GAS 4

CAKE

2 eggs

4 oz (115 g) butter or margarine

2 oz (60 g) soft brown sugar

2 tablespoons thick honey

6 oz (175 g) plain flour

$\frac{1}{2}$ oz (15 g) baking powder

4 tablespoons milk

TOPPING AND FILLING

3 oz (85 g) butter

3 oz (85 g) sieved icing sugar

$1\frac{1}{2}$ oz (45 g) flaked toasted almonds

$1\frac{1}{2}$ tablespoons thick honey

7" (20 cm) cake tin, lined – 2 bowls – sieve – 2 tablespoons – wooden spoon – knife – palette knife – whisk – cooling rack

CAKE

1 In one of the bowls beat the eggs lightly.

2 In the second bowl cream together the butter, sugar and honey to a soft and light consistency and then gently fold in the eggs.

3 Fold the sifted flour and baking powder into the mixture, adding the milk gradually.

4 Put the mixture into the prepared cake tin and bake in the centre of the oven for about 45 minutes.

5 Remove from the oven and allow to cool before placing on the cooling rack.

TOPPING AND FILLING

1 Cream the butter well before adding the sugar and honey.

  2 Cut through the centre of the cake and spread evenly with part of the honey butter cream.
  3 Spread the remaining honey butter cream over the top and sides of the cake and decorate it with the flaked almonds, pressing them into the cream.

Fudge Cake

Way back when — when I was at school — fudge cake was a rare and very special treat. It isn't hard to see why.

OVEN TEMPERATURE:
400°F/205°C/GAS 6

CAKE

2 egg yolks
1 oz (30 g) cocoa powder
3 tablespoons warm water
2½ oz (70 g) margarine, melted
5 oz (145 g) caster sugar
6 oz (175 g) plain flour
1½ teaspoons baking powder
4 tablespoons milk
a little lemon juice
½ teaspoon vanilla

TOPPING

2 egg whites
5 oz (145 g) soft light brown sugar
1 oz (30 g) chocolate dots
1 oz (30 g) chopped almonds
½ teaspoon baking powder

7" (20 cm) square cake tin — 4 bowls — jug — sieve — whisk — spatula — 2 tablespoons — teaspoon — sharp knife — fork — cooling rack — sheet of greaseproof paper

CAKE

  1 Separate the egg whites and yolks into two of the bowls.
  2 In the third bowl put the cocoa and water and blend well, then add the margarine and sugar, stirring all the time.
  3 Beat the egg yolks and add half a teaspoon of vanilla essence and add to chocolate mixture.
  4 Add a few drops of lemon juice to the milk in the jug to make it sour.
  5 Sieve together the flour and baking powder and stir into the chocolate mixture alternately with the milk, taking care to mix well.

6 Pour the mixture into the prepared cake tin and bake in the centre of the oven for 25 minutes.

TOPPING

1 Whisk the egg whites until stiff and lightly fold in the sugar, baking powder and chocolate dots.

2 Spoon the topping over the cake and sprinkle with the chopped nuts.

3 Cover the cake with the sheet of greaseproof paper and bake for a further 40 minutes at 360°F (180°C) Gas 4–5, until a skewer comes out clean when inserted into the centre.

4 Turn the cake out onto the cooling rack.

This cake should be eaten very fresh.

Brandy Snaps

Although I still see brandy snaps from time to time, neatly packed in boxes with 'window tops', in the supermarket and at the village grocer's, it is years since I was invited anywhere where they were served for tea. Of course, I could make some myself but somehow I never seem to get around to it.

OVEN TEMPERATURE:
310°F/155°C/GAS 2–3

1 oz (30 g) butter
2½ oz (70 g) caster sugar
1 oz (30 g) golden syrup
1 oz (30 g) plain flour
1 teaspoon ground ginger

bowl – baking sheet, greased – several wooden spoon handles or other similar wooden or metal rods, well greased – palette knife

1 Cream together the butter, sugar and syrup until smooth and evenly mixed.

2 Stir in the flour and ground ginger gently but thoroughly.

3 Make into about 14 equal sized balls.

4 Set well apart on the baking sheet, allowing plenty of room for spreading.

5 Bake for 10–15 minutes, until a rich golden brown.

6 Allow to cool a little for about 1 minute.

7 Remove from baking sheet with palette knife.

8 Roll round greased wooden spoon handle and allow to cool and set.

For filling see page 127.

Marbled Almond Cake

Marbled Almond Cake is always popular but it has never seemed to me that the result quite justifies the effort. I feel rather like Bernard Shaw on the occasion when he is reputed to have gone up to the only member of the audience not rapturously applauding one of his plays and said, 'I quite agree with you, sir, but who are we against so many!'

OVEN TEMPERATURE:
350°F/180°C/GAS 4

8 oz (230 g) butter
9 oz (255 g) caster sugar
6 oz (175 g) almond paste
5 egg yolks
1 teaspoon vanilla
12 egg whites
½ teaspoon salt
1 lb (460 g) plain flour
3 oz (85 g) semi-sweet chocolate, melted

2 × 1 lb (500 g) loaf tins – 3 bowls – 3 cups – 2 teaspoons – sieve – whisk – tablespoon – spatula – saucepan

1 Separate the egg whites and yolks into two of the bowls.
2 In the other bowl cream the butter with a quarter cup of sugar.
3 Add the almond paste, a little at a time, creaming it in well, until the mixture is light and fluffy.
4 Add the egg yolks one at a time, beating well after each one.
5 Pour the vanilla into the mixture.
6 Add the salt to the egg whites and beat until the white holds soft peaks.
7 Add the remaining sugar to the egg whites, a tablespoon at a time, continuing beating for 5 minutes or until the egg whites are very firm.
8 Stir a quarter of the stiffly beaten egg whites into the creamed almond paste mixture.
9 Pour this mixture back over the remaining egg whites.
10 Fold the mixtures together, whilst sprinkling in the sieved flour, as you fold.
11 Add the melted chocolate to the mixture and marble the chocolate roughly by drawing through it with a spatula.
12 Pour the mixture into the prepared tins.
13 Bake in a pre-set oven for 1 hour 15 minutes, or until the cakes are golden brown and pull away from the sides of the tin.

Devil's Food Cake

I am often puzzled about how cakes get their names. If this is really what the devil eats, then perhaps I regret my many sins a little less.

OVEN TEMPERATURE:
350°F/180°C/GAS 4

8 oz (230 g) granulated sugar
4 oz (115 g) cocoa powder
¾ pint (4.5 dl) sour milk
8 oz (230 g) plain flour
2 teaspoons baking powder
½ teaspoon salt
8 oz (230 g) caster sugar
4 oz (115 g) butter
2 eggs
few drops vanilla essence, to taste

9″ (25 cm) cake tin and a heat resistant jar or tin or 9″ (25 cm) savarin ring – 3 bowls – sieve – whisk – spatula

1 In one bowl mix together the granulated sugar, cocoa and ¼ pint (1.5 dl) of sour milk. Leave this to stand while the other ingredients are prepared.

2 Sift the flour, salt and baking powder together.

3 In the other bowl, cream together the eggs, caster sugar and butter until it is a light, almost white, fluffy mixture, remembering that over-beating can cause butter to separate.

4 Add the dry mix slowly and steadily.

5 Mixing continuously and steadily, pour in the remainder of the sour milk and the vanilla essence.

6 Add the cocoa and sugar mixture. Continue to beat until the mixture is a smooth, even consistency and colour.

7 Place the mixture in the cake tin or savarin ring, smoothing the top carefully. (Putting a heat resistant jar or tin in the centre of an ordinary cake tin can produce a result not unlike that of a savarin ring; naturally it is better to use the genuine article.)

8 Bake in the pre-set oven for about 1 hour until the cake is well set and a good even colour.

The hole in the centre can be filled with various creams described on pages 127–9 or with plain whipped cream decorated to taste.

Angel Cake

. . . on the other hand, if this is what the angels have to offer I wish I had been a whole lot more virtuous!

OVEN TEMPERATURE:
290°F/145°C/GAS ½–1

2 oz (60 g) plain flour
4½ oz (130 g) caster sugar
4 egg whites
a pinch of salt
½ teaspoon cream of tartar
few drops vanilla essence, to taste

6" (15 cm) cake tin, greased – bowl – fine sieve – whisk – kitchen knife

1 Sift the flour several times. It cannot be too fine in this recipe.
2 Sift the caster sugar several times as the same applies. (I have seen it suggested that icing sugar be used but there is the danger that it will revert too easily to lumps. If you are extra careful, however, you could try using it, sifting it first.)
3 Sift the flour and a quarter of the sugar together.
4 In the bowl add the salt to the egg whites and whisk till they are firm and fluffy. Do not over beat as this will make the egg white fall back into a rather nasty mess.
5 Sprinkle the cream of tartar onto this and continue to beat until the mixture will support clearly defined peaks. Do not over beat.
6 Very lightly beat in the remaining sugar and the vanilla essence. Beat just enough to make the mixture even in consistency.
7 Fold in the flour and sugar mix very gently.
8 Cut through the mixture several times with the knife to get rid of any air bubbles.
9 Put mixture into the cake tin, cut through it again just to make sure, and place in the pre-set oven for between 45 minutes and 1 hour until it is fairly well set.
10 Increase the oven heat to 335°F (170°C) Gas 3–4 and bake for another 15 minutes.
11 Remove from the oven and turn the tin upside down and leave to cool for about half an hour, preferably on a cooling rack. (If the cake falls out, never mind. It can cool just as well standing on its head.)
12 Remove the cake from the tin and let it finish cooling.

Marillenkuchen

I am told that this cake is much better when made with fresh apricots than with tinned ones. I can't be sure. What happens is that I buy a couple of pounds of apricots to make the cake and as the recipe calls for only half a pound it occurs to me that it won't hurt if I eat one or two. By the time it gets to putting the apricots on the cake the bag is empty! Next time I buy four pounds of apricots and the same thing happens. Tinned apricots are very good, but I can just about resist them.

OVEN TEMPERATURE:
350°F/175°C/GAS 4

4 large eggs
5 oz (145 g) butter
8 oz (230 g) caster sugar
6 oz (175 g) plain flour
8 oz (230 g) fresh apricots
   or 15 oz (430 g) tinned and drained apricots
a little icing sugar

swiss roll tin 13″ × 8½″ × 1½″ deep, greased and floured – 3 bowls – whisk – spatula – sieve – sharp knife

1 Separate the egg whites and yolks into two of the bowls.
2 In the third bowl cream the butter and sugar together, well but gently, taking care not to over beat. Beat in egg yolks.
3 Whisk the egg whites until they are stiff and fold into the butter and egg mixture. Gradually add the sifted flour and mix well together.
4 Spread the mixture evenly onto the prepared cake tin.
5 If using fresh apricots, cut with a sharp knife in half and remove the stones, placing them at even intervals over the mixture.
6 Bake in the pre-set oven for 1 hour until it is a golden brown colour.
7 Remove from the oven and allow to cool.
8 Dust with icing sugar before serving.

Streusel Cake

This cake is a great favourite in Germany from where it comes. One of the great mysteries to me is how it is possible to eat streusel cake, as many Germans do, after an enormous Christmas dinner. In the first place it is a bit on the filling side and in the second place it is impossible to eat only one slice . . .

CAKE
8 oz (230 g) plain flour
1 oz (30 g) caster sugar
½ oz (15 g) yeast
2 oz (60 g) butter
1 egg
¼ pint (1.5 dl) milk
a pinch of salt
FILLING
2 oz (60 g) plain flour
2 oz (60 g) caster sugar
2 oz (60 g) butter

OVEN TEMPERATURE:
360°F/185°C/GAS 4–5

bowl – 1 lb (500 g) bread tin – cloth – pastry board, floured – sieve – wooden spoon

CAKE
1 Sift the flour and salt into a bowl.
2 Mix together the yeast and sugar.
3 Add this to the flour, mixing thoroughly.
4 Slightly warm the butter to soften and add this to the flour.
5 Add the egg and the milk (preferably slightly warmed).
6 Mix all this together until it is completely smooth.
7 Place in a warm spot to rise until it has doubled in size (30–45 minutes).
8 Put the dough onto a floured pastry board, knead it thoroughly but not roughly.
9 Mould into shape of a loaf.
10 Place in the bread tin (greased) which it should fill to about a quarter of its depth.

FILLING
1 Sieve the flour into the bowl and mix in the sugar.
2 Melt the butter. Do not let it separate.
3 Pour the melted butter into the flour and sugar mixture and work together with fingers until crumbly.
4 Spread this mixture on top of the cake.
5 Bake in pre-heated oven for 35–40 minutes.

Gâteaux

During the last war my brother was trapped in Europe. When I managed to re-establish contact with him after the end of the war he had managed to get to Paris. I was able to 'con' the Navy into giving me permission to visit him. I thought, accurately, as it turned out, that the good things in life might be in short supply over there and decided to take a few such luxuries as were available here at the time to give him. The trip was filled with incidents among which I remember particularly my meeting with a French Customs official who pointed suspiciously at one of my many packages and asked what was in it. I stood there stammering and stuttering while I frantically searched my memory for the French word for 'Gâteau'!

There must be sound linguistic reasons why so many English culinary terms are borrowed from the French; why a sheep becomes mutton, why a pig becomes pork and why dead cattle are labelled 'beef'. Why certain confections are called gâteaux does not matter too much, what is important is that gâteaux exist, and in an infinite variety. It would, I suppose, be possible for a team of dedicated researchers to compile a complete catalogue of the world's gâteaux – but it would run into several volumes. I don't pretend, then, that the few recipes I have selected are anywhere near exhaustive or even representative. I hope, however, that I have managed to give some slight idea of the many deliciously fancy cakes that can be made under the generic heading of 'gâteaux' and, better still, that I may have inspired you to invent one of your own.

Chocolate Gâteau

Chocolate gâteau is the most popular of all gâteaux and at its best the most rare. Deceptively simple to make it can turn out the most delectable or the dullest of cakes. Unless you are prepared to take time and trouble I'd suggest that you turn to something else.

OVEN TEMPERATURE:
350°F/175°C/GAS 4

GÂTEAU
2½ oz (70 g) semi-sweet chocolate
3½ oz (100 g) unsweetened chocolate
8 eggs
8 oz (230 g) caster sugar
5 oz (145 g) plain flour
2 or 3 drops vanilla essence
chocolate vermicelli for decoration

FILLING
2 egg yolks
⅛ pint (0.75 dl) water
3 oz (85 g) caster sugar
3 oz (85 g) softened butter
½ oz (15 g) cocoa powder

7" or 8" (20 cm) cake tin (line the bottom with wax paper and grease and flour the sides) – 5 bowls – whisk – spatula – palette knife – sharp knife – saucepan – wooden spoon – cooling rack

GÂTEAU
1 Put the chocolate in a bowl and melt over warm water.
2 In the second bowl whisk the eggs with the sugar and vanilla until they are thick – you may find it is easier to do this over warm water.
3 Add the flour slowly to the eggs and sugar, still beating carefully.
4 Add the melted chocolate and mix quickly but carefully together until the ingredients are evenly mixed.
5 Pour the mixture into the prepared cake tin and smooth over with the palette knife to get an even surface.
6 Bake in the pre-set oven for 35–40 minutes.
7 Remove from the oven and turn the cake out onto the cooling rack and allow to go cold.
8 When the cake is cold, cut across the middle horizontally with the sharp knife, ready for the chocolate filling to be added.

FILLING AND DECORATION
1 Separate the egg yolks from the whites into two of the bowls.
2 Put the water into the saucepan, add the sugar

and gently bring to the boil, stirring all the time until it forms a 'thread' when the spoon is removed from the saucepan. Continue stirring until it becomes thick and syrupy and remove from heat.

3 Add the egg yolks slowly, mixing thoroughly together. Continue stirring until the mixture is really thick.

4 In another bowl cream the softened butter until it becomes very creamy and white – it needs to be firmly whipped until it is smooth.

5 Add the butter to the egg and sugar mixture, mixing well but lightly, then add the cocoa powder.

6 Spread some of the chocolate cream filling onto the bottom half of the gâteau evenly with the palette knife. Then place the other half of the gâteau on top of the cream filling and cover the top and sides of the gâteau with what remains.

7 To give the gâteau a finished look, decorate the top and sides with chocolate vermicelli or, if you prefer, pipe little chocolate shells around the gâteau with some of the cream filling.

Coffee Cream Gâteau

Coffee gâteau runs neck and neck with chocolate gâteau in the popularity stakes – at least with adults. Be very careful mixing the cream filling, you may want to increase or decrease the coffee powder or the sugar by a fraction. Personally, I like to grate a little orange peel into the cream but this may not be to everyone's taste.

GÂTEAU
8 eggs
9 oz (255 g) caster sugar
5 oz (145 g) finely chopped almonds
5 oz (145 g) plain flour
a few coffee beans for decoration
FILLING
6 egg yolks
9 oz (255 g) caster sugar
1 oz (30 g) coffee powder
6 oz (175 g) butter
2 or 3 drops vanilla essence

cake tin, greased and floured – 2 bowls – whisk – spatula – palette knife – sharp knife – saucepan – cooling tray

OVEN TEMPERATURE:
350°F/175°C/GAS 4

GÂTEAU

1 Separate the egg yolks and whites in the two bowls.

2 Add the sugar to the egg yolks and whisk until very creamy.

3 Chop the almonds and add to the egg yolks and sugar mixture, then add the flour and mix well but gently.

4 Whisk the egg whites very stiffly and add to the mixture.

5 Put the mixture in the prepared cake tin and bake in the pre-set oven for 30 minutes.

6 Remove from the oven and turn out onto the cooling tray.

7 When the cake is cold, cut horizontally, ready for the filling.

FILLING AND DECORATION

1 Mix the egg yolks and sugar together in one of the bowls until a smooth mixture is obtained.

2 Add the coffee powder to the egg and sugar mixture.

3 Boil some water in a saucepan and put the bowl with the egg and sugar mixture on top of the water, stirring all the time until it becomes smooth and creamy.

4 Remove from the heat but continue to stir until it is cool.

5 In another bowl beat the butter until it is smooth and white.

6 Add the beaten butter to the egg and sugar mixture and stir in the vanilla.

7 Spread some of the cream filling evenly on the bottom layer of the cake with the palette knife. Then put the other layer on top and spread the remainder of the cream evenly over the top and sides of the gâteau, taking great care to finish this part neatly and smoothly.

8 Decorate the top and sides with the coffee beans.

Orange Gâteau

When the famous Rossini opera,
The Barber of Seville, *had its
very first performance in 1816 the
audience hissed, and quite right
too. Oh yes, the music is
enchanting and Sterbini's libretto
witty, but why carry on about a
barber when Seville produces such
magnificent oranges!*

OVEN TEMPERATURE:
350°F/175°C/GAS 4

GÂTEAU
6 eggs
6 oz (175 g) caster sugar
8 oz (230 g) ground almonds
grated rind of 3 oranges
juice of 1½ oranges
3 teaspoons cake crumbs
FILLING
3 egg yolks
9 oz (255 g) butter
6 oz (175 g) caster sugar
grated peel of 2 oranges
1 small orange and/or a little orange jelly for
  decoration

3 × 8" (20 cm) shallow cake tins, greased –
2 bowls – whisk – grater – grinder – fruit juice
squeezer – palette knife – spatula – cooling tray

GÂTEAU
  1 Separate the egg yolks and whites into two of
    the bowls.
  2 Whisk the egg yolks and sugar together until
    they are creamy.
  3 Add the ground almonds, orange juice, grated
    peel and cake crumbs to the egg and sugar
    mixture and mix well together.
  4 Whisk the egg whites until they are very stiff
    and carefully fold them into the mixture.
  5 Pour the mixture into the prepared tins,
    spreading an equal quantity evenly into each
    tin and bake in the pre-set oven for 15–18
    minutes.
  6 Remove from the oven and turn out onto the
    cooling rack.
  7 Wash all your equipment so you can use it for
    the next stage.
FILLING AND DECORATION
  1 Separate the egg yolks.
  2 Put the butter and sugar into a bowl and beat
    until light and creamy, taking great care not
    to over beat.
  3 Add the egg yolks gradually to the butter and
    sugar and continue to stir, slowly adding the

grated orange peel. Mix all the ingredients together thoroughly until the mixture becomes stiff and hard.

4 Spread the cream filling onto each layer of the sandwich cake and finally spread some of the cream around the sides.

5 As a finishing touch you can decorate the top of the cake with pieces of orange or, if you prefer, you can use orange jelly and orange rind.

Date Gâteau

I am told that it takes about eight years for a date palm to bear its first fruit. As without dates we could not make this rich and succulent gâteau, the wait doesn't seem any too long!

OVEN TEMPERATURE:
375°F/190°C/GAS 5

GÂTEAU
4 eggs
4 oz (115 g) caster sugar
5 oz (145 g) shredded or grated almonds
5 oz (145 g) chopped dates
FILLING
½ pint (3 dl) whipping cream
a little caster sugar
a few drops vanilla essence
a few chopped dates for decoration

cake tin – 2 bowls – whisk – grater – sharp knife – palette knife

GÂTEAU

1 Separate the egg yolks and whites into two bowls.

2 Add the sugar to the egg yolks and beat well.

3 Add the almonds and dates to the sugar and egg mixture and mix well together.

4 Whisk the egg whites until they are very stiff and add them carefully and lightly to the mixture, a little at a time.

5 Pour the mixture into the prepared cake tin and bake in the pre-set oven until golden brown.

6 Remove from the oven and turn out on to the cooling tray.

7 Allow to go cold, then cut across the middle of the gâteau horizontally with a sharp knife.

FILLING AND DECORATION

1 Whip the cream and sugar together and add a little vanilla for flavouring.
2 Spread the cream onto the bottom half of the gâteau and put the other half on top.
3 Decorate the gâteau with remains of chopped dates.

Delicious Gâteau

There is Chocolate Gâteau. There is Coffee Gâteau. There is Orange Gâteau. This is a recipe for Delicious Gâteau *– what more is there to say!*

OVEN TEMPERATURE:
350°F/175°C/GAS 4

GÂTEAU

7 eggs
9 oz (255 g) caster sugar
9 oz (255 g) ground walnuts
25 roasted coffee beans ground fairly finely
a few drops vanilla essence
a few blanched almonds for decorating

FILLING

5 oz (145 g) butter
6 oz (175 g) bitter chocolate, melted
3 oz (85 g) caster sugar
3 egg yolks

8" (20 cm) round cake tin – 4 bowls – whisk – grinder – spatula – palette knife – sharp knife – cooling rack

GÂTEAU

1 Put the eggs and sugar into a bowl and beat with a whisk until very creamy and fluffy.
2 Add the ground walnuts, coffee beans and vanilla to the egg mixture, mixing all together thoroughly but lightly.
3 Pour the mixture into the prepared cake tin and bake in the pre-set oven for 40 minutes.
4 Remove from the oven and turn out on to the cooling rack.
5 When the cake is cold cut across the middle horizontally and leave ready for the filling.

FILLING AND DECORATION

1 Melt the chocolate and butter together in a bowl by placing the bowl inside another bowl containing hot water.
2 Add the egg yolks and sugar slowly to the

Simnel Cake *page 113*
Gugelhupf *page 63*
Marillenkuchen *page 72*

chocolate and butter mixture, stirring over the hot water until the mixture becomes thick.

3 Remove the bowl from the hot water and allow the mixture to cool.

4 Spread half of the chocolate cream evenly on one layer of the gâteau. Then place the other layer on top and spread the remainder of the cream on top of it.

5 Decorate the gâteau with blanched almonds or cake crumbs.

Nuss Torte

Most people like walnuts and almonds and you will find that this nut cake is suitable for almost any occasion.

OVEN TEMPERATURE: 350°F/175°C/GAS 4

TORTE

7 eggs

5 oz (145 g) caster sugar

2 oz (60 g) fine, dry white breadcrumbs

3 oz (85 g) chopped walnuts and toasted almonds, mixed

a few drops vanilla essence

a few whole walnuts for decoration

ICING

3 eggs

6 oz (175 g) caster sugar

2 oz (60 g) unsweetened chocolate, melted

a few drops vanilla essence

3 × 8″ (20 cm) sandwich tins, greased – 3 bowls – whisk – spatula – sharp knife – cooling tray – double saucepan

TORTE

1 Separate the egg yolks and whites into two bowls.

2 Add the sugar to the egg yolk and whisk until thick and creamy.

3 Whisk the egg whites until they are stiff.

4 Add the vanilla essence to the egg and sugar mixture.

5 Mix the breadcrumbs and finely chopped mixed nuts together and fold them into the egg and sugar mixture, then gradually add the beaten egg whites.

6 Pour the mixture in equal proportions into

the 3 sandwich tins and bake in the pre-set oven for 25 minutes until they are firm and golden brown.

7 Allow the cakes to cool before turning them on to the cooling rack.

ICING

1 Put the eggs and sugar into the double saucepan and stir until the mixture begins to thicken, taking great care not to overheat as this will cause it to curdle.

2 Remove from the heat and stir in the previously melted chocolate, add the vanilla essence and beat the mixture until it is well mixed and really thick. Allow to cool.

3 Divide the filling between each layer and cover the top of the cake with what remains. Then decorate with the whole walnuts.

Chestnut Gâteau

If you really want to impress your guests you can call this Gâteau aux Marrons. Either way, it tastes delicious.

OVEN TEMPERATURE:
350°F/175°C/GAS 4

6 eggs
11 oz (315 g) caster sugar
12 oz (345 g) chestnuts
2 oz (60 g) grated hazelnuts
a few drops vanilla essence
½ pint (3 dl) fresh whipped cream for filling
2 oz (60 g) chopped chestnuts for decoration

round cake tin 7″ (20 cm) – saucepan – sieve – whisk – grater – spatula – sharp knife – cooling tray – 4 bowls

1 Separate the egg whites and yolks into the two bowls.

2 Peel the chestnuts and put them to boil until they are soft. Remove from the heat, strain off the water and pass the chestnuts through a sieve into another bowl.

3 Whisk the egg yolks and sugar together thoroughly.

4 Add the sieved chestnuts to the egg yolks and sugar.

5 Add the finely grated hazelnuts to the egg yolk mixture, then add a little vanilla.

6 Whisk the egg whites until stiff and fluffy.

7 Very carefully add the stiffly whisked egg whites to the mixture.

8 Pour the mixture into the cake tin and bake in the pre-set oven.

9 Remove from the oven and allow to cool on the cooling tray.

10 When cool, cut across the gâteau horizontally and spread evenly with fresh cream – to which you first add a drop or two of vanilla – using the palette knife.

11 Decorate the top of the gâteau with the chopped chestnuts.

Gâteau Edouard

A restaurant in Paris in the 1870s or 1880s. The Prince of Wales and a young lady in a 'chambre privée'. The young lady is disappointed, disgruntled, possibly even disgusted. It seems as if His Royal Highness has forgotten all about her. Ever since that gâteau was served she has been unable to distract his attention from it – and she is a most attractive young lady indeed. At last, there's not a crumb of gâteau left and . . .

This splendid gâteau is named after that Prince of Wales whose appetite for the good things in life remains legendary in the Paris that he loved.

OVEN TEMPERATURE:
350°F/175°C/GAS 4

GATEAU
5 eggs
5 oz (145 g) caster sugar
5 oz (145 g) butter
4 oz (115 g) unsweetened chocolate
2 oz (60 g) ground almonds
1 teaspoon breadcrumbs
1 teaspoon finely ground coffee
¼ pint (1.5 dl) double cream, whipped
2 oz (60 g) roasted chopped almonds for decoration

FILLING
3 egg yolks
1 oz (30 g) caster sugar
¼ pint (1.5 dl) strong black coffee
  or 1 teaspoon of coffee powder dissolved in
  1 tbs hot water
5 oz (145 g) butter, softened

cake tin, greased and floured – 3 bowls – grinder – whisk – spatula – palette knife – 2 teaspoons – saucepan – cooling rack

GÂTEAU
1 Separate the egg yolks and whites into two of the bowls.

2 Cream the egg yolks, sugar and butter together.

3 Melt the chocolate in another bowl over hot water and add to the egg and butter mixture.

4 Add the breadcrumbs, ground almonds and ground coffee to the mixture and blend well together.

5 Beat the egg whites until they are very stiff, then fold them gently into the mixture.

6 Put the mixture into the prepared cake tin and bake in the pre-set oven for 25–28 minutes.

7 Remove from the oven and turn out on to the cooling rack. When cold cut across horizontally into three equal layers.

8 Wash all the equipment for use in making the filling.

FILLING AND DECORATION

1 Put the egg yolks, sugar and coffee into a bowl.

2 Place the bowl over a saucepan of slowly boiling water and whisk the cream well until it becomes smooth and thick.

3 Remove the bowl from the hot water but continue whisking until the cream cools.

4 Add the softened butter to the cream and mix well together.

5 On the bottom layer of the gâteau spread some of the cream filling evenly, then put another layer of gâteau on top and repeat until all three of the layers have been used.

6 Cover the top of the gâteau with the piped double whipped cream and decorate the sides with the chopped almonds.

Millefeuille Gâteau

Sheer luxury. But it must be kept in the refrigerator for a while before serving and make sure you have a very sharp pointed knife to cut it.

PASTRY
as for puff pastry (see page 134)
FILLING
a little lemon icing (see page 132)
½ pint fresh whipped cream
sugar to taste
½ lb strawberries
a little redcurrant jelly

pastry board – rolling pin – bowl – palette knife – baking sheet – fork – whisk

OVEN TEMPERATURE:
425°F/220°C/GAS 7

PASTRY

1 Make as for puff pastry (see pages 134–5).
2 Roll the pastry out thinly and cut out six rounds 7″ (17¾ cm) in diameter, then prick them firmly with a fork.
3 Place the rounds on to the damp baking sheet and bake in the oven until they are a light golden brown colour.
5 Remove from the oven and allow to cool.

FILLING AND TOPPING

1 Slice ½ the strawberries and mix with ½ the whipped cream.
2 Build up the layers with the strawberry filling.
3 Place the remaining strawberries in halves on the top and glaze with melted redcurrant jelly.
4 Pipe with the remaining cream.

Carlton Millefeuille Gâteau

Even grander than the previous recipe but you must observe the same rules. The millefeuille should be served cold from the fridge and unless it is cut with a very sharp knife it will be transformed into a disappointing, squidgy mess.

OVEN TEMPERATURE:
425°F/220°C/GAS 7

PASTRY
as for puff pastry (see page 134)

FILLING AND TOPPING
whipped cream, flavoured with coffee or chocolate if desired
fresh cream or water icing
roasted almonds or hazelnuts, chopped

bowl – sieve – rolling pin – pastry board – whisk – sharp knife – baking sheet

PASTRY

1 Make as for puff pastry (see pages 134–5).
2 Cut into four 8″ rounds and bake in a hot oven.

FILLING AND TOPPING

1 The whipped cream may be left plain or flavoured with coffee, chocolate or vanilla and placed on a round of the pastry.
2 Repeat until all the rounds have been used, then cover the gâteau with fresh cream or water icing and decorate with the finely chopped almonds or hazelnuts.

Morello Cherry Gâteau

It was the Roman general, Lucius Lucullus, who first brought the cherry to Europe from Asia which was its natural home. We should be grateful to him. All cherries, and most particularly the Morello cherry, add to the taste pleasures of life.

OVEN TEMPERATURE:
375°F/190°C/GAS 5

GÂTEAU
3 eggs
2½ oz (70 g) unsweetened chocolate
3 oz (85 g) caster sugar
2 oz (60 g) plain flour
3 oz (85 g) melted butter
FILLING
1 egg yolk
3½ oz (100 g) caster sugar
1 oz (30 g) unsweetened chocolate
4 oz (115 g) butter
6 oz (175 g) stewed morello cherries
a drop of brandy

8″ cake tin, greased and floured – 3 bowls – whisk – grater – spatula – palette knife – sharp knife – cooling rack – saucepan

GÂTEAU
1 Separate the egg yolks and whites into two of the bowls.
2 Grate the chocolate in the third bowl and put in a warm place to melt.
3 Add half the sugar to the egg yolks and beat well.
4 Whisk the egg whites stiffly and gradually fold in the remainder of the sugar.
5 Fold the egg whites gently into the egg yolk mixture.
6 Add the flour, melted butter and grated chocolate to the mixture and mix well together.
7 Pour the mixture into the prepared cake tin and bake in the pre-set oven for 40 minutes.
8 Remove from the oven and place on the cooling rack.
9 When cold, cut through the middle horizontally with a sharp knife.
FILLING AND DECORATION
1 Put the egg yolk and sugar into a bowl, place the bowl over another containing steaming hot water, whisk the mixture until it thickens.

2 Melt the chocolate in the saucepan and add it to the egg mixture then add the butter and brandy and mix well together.

3 Cut about two thirds of the cherries into fairly small pieces.

4 Spread some chocolate filling on the bottom layer of gâteau, then place another layer of cake over the top.

5 Mix a little of the filling with the chopped cherries and spread over the second layer of sponge. Then cover with the third layer of sponge.

6 Spread some chocolate filling over the sides of the cake and coat with chocolate vermicelli.

7 Place some filling in a piping bag fitted with a fluted nozzle and use the remaining icing to cover the top of the cake. Mark with a palette knife, then pipe around the edges and decorate with the whole cherries.

Calypso Gâteau

When the weather is persistently bad, when the boss has been even more unreasonable than usual, when young Jimmy has come home drunk for the fourth time in a week (and it's only Tuesday) make a Calypso Gâteau and, as you take your first bite out of it, you'll fancy you are on a beach, in front of a luxury hotel, with the waves breaking invitingly and not even the smallest cloud to punctuate the perfect blue of the sky.

OVEN TEMPERATURE:
375°F/190°C/GAS 5

CAKE
6 oz (175 g) butter
6 oz (175 g) caster sugar
4 oz (115 g) black treacle
3 eggs
2 oz (60 g) cornflour
6 oz (175 g) plain flour
1½ teaspoons baking powder
3 tablespoons milk

FILLING
8 oz (230 g) butter
12 oz (345 g) icing sugar
2 oz (60 g) black treacle
½ wine glass of rum, more or less, to taste
4 tablespoons milk
4 tablespoons hot water
2–3 oz (60–85 g) half walnuts for decoration

2 × 7" (20 cm) cake tins, lined or greased – bowl – sieve – whisk – wooden spoon – sharp knife – palette knife – fork – 3 glasses or cups

1 Whisk together the butter, sugar and treacle until the texture is smooth and light.
2 Beat in the eggs, one at a time, adding a sprinkling of flour if the mixture shows signs of curdling.
3 Sift the cornflour, flour and baking powder into the mixture and fold in.
4 Mix in the milk.
5 Divide mixture equally into two cake tins and bake for 25–30 minutes. (Test by finger pressure – if no dent is left cake is cooked.)
6 While cake is baking, prepare filling by beating the butter, icing sugar and treacle together until smooth and creamy. Add the rum, milk and water (in that order) a little at a time, beating continuously.
7 As soon as the cakes are cool enough, cut both into half horizontally to make four layers.
8 Spread each layer with rum butter and sandwich them together.
9 Cover the whole with the remainder of the rum butter and mark this with wavy lines made with the fork.
10 Decorate with the half walnuts.

Linzer Torte

In Austria, on the banks of Strauss's Danube, is the substantial city of Linz. This is where Hitler lived as a boy. It is also the home town of the Linzer torte.

OVEN TEMPERATURE:
370°F/190°C/GAS 4–5

1 egg
1 egg yolk
6 oz (175 g) plain flour
4 oz (115 g) butter
4 oz (115 g) caster sugar
4 oz (115 g) almonds or walnuts, grated
rind of 1 lemon, grated
a little cinnamon
a little of your favourite jam
a little redcurrant jelly
salt

10″ flan ring, greased – bowl – whisk – pastry board – rolling pin – pastry brush – knife – sieve

1 Put the whole egg and extra egg yolk into the bowl.

2 Sieve the flour on to the pastry board with a little cinnamon and a pinch of salt.

3 Make a well in the centre of the flour and put in it the butter, sugar, egg and grated lemon rind.

4 Add the grated almonds or walnuts.

5 Mix together well with the finger tips until it is a smooth texture then roll into a ball and leave for about 1 hour in a cool place.

6 Roll the paste at least $\frac{1}{2}"$ ($1\frac{1}{4}$ cm) thick and line the prepared flan ring, leaving aside a small amount of the paste.

7 Add a little sugar to the jam, mix well – heating it a little if necessary, and pour into the flan ring.

8 Roll the remaining paste out very thinly and cut into strips.

9 Put the strips of paste in a criss-cross pattern over the top for decoration and brush with egg yolk.

10 Bake in the pre-set oven for about 25–30 minutes.

11 When cool, brush over with the redcurrant jelly which you have warmed a little so that it spreads easily.

Nurnbergi Torta

It is said that the Hungarians are generous. What better proof could there be than their creating this superb gâteau and then naming it after a Bavarian town!

OVEN TEMPERATURE:
350°F/175°C/GAS 4

8 eggs
6 oz (175 g) caster sugar
5 oz (145 g) walnuts
8 oz (230 g) unsweetened chocolate
2 oz (60 g) cake crumbs
a little sweetened double cream
a little chocolate ⎰
a little milk ⎱ for decoration

3 bowls – spatula – whisk – cooling rack – baking trays, greased

1 Separate the egg yolks and whites into two of the bowls.

2 Put all the dry ingredients into another bowl and add the egg yolks. These are not whisked separately.

3 Whisk the egg whites.
4 Mix all the ingredients together thoroughly but gently.
5 Pour the mixture on to the prepared baking trays and bake in the pre-set oven until it is a golden-beige colour, about 15–20 minutes.
6 Remove from the oven and place on the cooling rack.
7 Whisk or beat the cream with a little sugar until it is very thick then spread an equal quantity between each layer of the cake with the palette knife until you have used all the layers.
8 Melt the chocolate, with a little warm milk, just sufficiently to be able to pour it over the cake. Allow it to set.

Fourré Gâteau

To be pedantic this gâteau should be called 'Gâteau Fourré'. It is a circular box made of an excellent sponge and filled with a rich and original cream.

OVEN TEMPERATURE:
350°F/175°C/GAS 4

GÂTEAU
4 oz (115 g) marzipan
8 oz (230 g) caster sugar
5 eggs
6 oz (175 g) plain flour
FILLING
1 oz (30 g) glacé cherries
2½ oz (70 g) sultanas
¼ pint (1.5 dl) custard (see page 129)
1 pint (5.5 dl) whipping cream
2 nips rum
a little jam
white fondant icing (see page 130)
roasted flaked almonds
1 oz (30 g) caster sugar

2 × 9" (25 cm) sandwich tins – 4 bowls – spatula – palette knife – sharp knife – whisk – 7" (20 cm) cutter or 7" (20 cm) plate and a sharp pointed knife – cooling rack

GÂTEAU
1 Put the marzipan into one of the bowls and melt with a little warm water.

2 Add the sugar and eggs and whisk together until light and fluffy.

3 Add the flour gradually and gently fold into the mixture.

4 Put the mixture in equal quantities into the two prepared sandwich tins.

5 Bake in the pre-set oven for 30 minutes.

6 Remove from the oven and turn out on to the cooling rack.

FILLING, TOPPING AND DECORATION

1 Set aside three cherries and a dozen sultanas for decoration.

2 Soak the remainder of the cherries and sultanas in the rum (if possible leave these to soak overnight).

3 Add the fresh cream to the cold custard and mix gently, then add the soaked drained fruits and rum.

4 Cut one of the sponge cakes across the middle horizontally.

5 Out of the centre of the other cake cut a 7″ (20 cm) disc and save it for decoration later.

6 Place the remaining 9″ (25 cm) ring on to one half of the cut sponge and fill the centre of the ring with some of the cream filling.

7 Put the top of the sandwich over the cream filling and cover the sides with the remainder.

8 Press the flaked nuts to the creamed sides of the gâteau.

9 Spread some jam evenly on top of the gâteau and cover with white fondant icing.

10 Chop the cherries and sultanas which have been left aside and sprinkle on to the fondant icing while it is still soft.

11 If you wish you can use the remaining 7″ (20 cm) ring of the sandwich by cutting it into 8–12 slices and placing them on top of the gâteau as decoration, dusting them with a little icing sugar.

Bohemian Gâteau

This is not an easy gâteau to make but it's well worth the trouble. Don't panic if the layers get crisp and biscuity – they're supposed to. It is a good idea to mention this otherwise someone will mutter something about the sponge being 'dry'. Another name for this gâteau, by the way, is 'La Bohème'.

OVEN TEMPERATURE:
350°F/175°C/GAS 4

10 egg whites
8 oz (230 g) caster sugar
3 oz (85 g) plain flour
3 oz (85 g) ground hazelnuts
3 oz (85 g) grated unsweetened chocolate
chocolate flavoured butter cream
praline flavoured butter cream
melted chocolate

baking tray or sheet, bakewell or silicone paper – 5 bowls – whisk – 8" (20 cm) cutter or 8" (20 cm) plate and a sharp pointed knife – palette knife – spatula – icing bag

1 Separate the egg whites and yolks into two of the bowls.
2 Add the sugar to the egg whites and whisk until stiff.
3 Add the flour, ground hazelnuts and grated chocolate to the egg whites and mix gently.
4 Spread the mixture into 8" circles about ¼" (½ cm) thick on the silicone paper.
5 Bake in the pre-set oven until lightly browned, i.e. for about 20 minutes.
6 Remove from the oven and allow to cool a bit, then remove from the paper carefully.
7 Re-use the silicone paper and make 6–8 rounds as the oven becomes free.
8 Spread a layer of chocolate butter cream evenly on one of the circles, then place another on top and cover with some of the praline butter cream. Go on building up the gâteau with alternate layers of the two different creams until all the circles have been used.
9 To finish the gâteau, pipe strands of melted chocolate over the top.

Sacher Torte

*This superb cake was created in
nineteenth-century Vienna by
Madame Sacher for her élite
clientele. It in no way damaged her
reputation as one of the world's
great pastry cooks!*

OVEN TEMPERATURE:
325°F/160°C/GAS 3

6 eggs
8 oz (230 g) unsweetened chocolate
3 oz (85 g) butter
8 oz (230 g) caster sugar
10 oz (285 g) plain flour
1 tablespoon water
a pinch of salt
4–6 oz (115–175 g) raspberry jam

8″ (20 cm) cake tin, greased or lined – 2 bowls –
double saucepan – sieve – whisk – palette knife

1 Separate the eggs into yolks and whites.
2 Add the pinch of salt to the egg whites and whisk until stiff.
3 Break 5 oz (145 g) of the chocolate into the top part of the double saucepan, add the tablespoon of water and heat gently over boiling water until the chocolate is melted, stirring steadily all the time.
4 Add the butter and stir until that too has melted.
5 Add the beaten egg yolks, whisking steadily until they are thoroughly mixed in.
6 Now add the sugar and again whisk until well mixed in.
7 Allow this mixture to cool for about 10–15 minutes.
8 While it is cooling, carefully sift the flour.
9 Fold the chocolate mixture and the flour, a little at a time, alternately into the egg whites, doing this gently but thoroughly.
10 Put the mixture into the prepared cake tin and put into the pre-heated oven for about 55 minutes or until a knife or skewer can be stuck into it and come out clean. This is a much heavier mixture than the conventional sponge and will, therefore, not rise as much and is meant to be much closer knit.
11 As soon as the sponge is baked, remove it from the cake tin and allow it to cool on a rack.
12 Melt the raspberry jam – a little water may be added and the jam may be sieved if you want to get rid of the pips.

13 When the sponge is thoroughly cool, cut it horizontally into two layers.

14 Spread the jam generously on both layers and put them together so that there is jam both in the middle and on top.

15 Melt the remainder of the chocolate in the double saucepan and spread this thinly and evenly over the top and sides of the cake.

16 The final touch is the piping of the word 'Sacher' in a darker chocolate on the top but I beg you not to attempt this your first time. Wait until you get results that will do honour to the memory of that fine cook.

Gâteau Saint Honoré

Make this gâteau with due reverence for St Honoré is the patron saint of bakers. When you taste it you will understand why it was this gâteau in particular that was honoured with his name.

OVEN TEMPERATURE:
475°F/245°C/GAS 9

1 lb (460 g) chou paste (see page 136)
1 pint (5.5 dl) whipped cream
a few drops vanilla essence
glacé cherries
angelica

2 baking trays, greased – 2 bowls – piping-bag – fork – spatula – whisk – sharp knife – saucepan – cooling rack

1 Prepare the chou paste as on page 136.

2 Using some of the paste, pipe it directly on to one baking tray to make a flat, round base 7″ (20 cm) in diameter.

3 Using the rest of the paste, pipe it in small round balls on to the other baking tray.

4 Bake in the pre-set oven for about 25 minutes or until golden brown.

5 Remove both the trays from the oven and prick the cakes with a fork to allow the steam to escape, then leave to cool.

6 Add a little vanilla to the cream and whip until it is thick.

7 Put some of the whipped cream into the balls and stick these on the chou base with a little warmed apricot jam.

8 With the remaining cream fill in the hollow part of the main cake round.

9 Decorate with pieces of glacé cherry and angelica.

The photograph of the finished product (see page 97) may help you see your way through this one and should act as an incentive too!

Gâteau Strips

For large parties, fêtes and that sort of occasion, where you will need to cut neat, regular portions quickly, to have the gâteau in strip form can be a great help.

For ingredients you will turn to the gâteau you have chosen to make, except that you may wish to double or treble the quantities. You'll also need more equipment and a baking sheet as big as your oven will comfortably take.

1 For mixing and baking follow the recipe you have selected.
2 After the sponge has cooled, cut into two horizontally. This is quite a tricky job till you have the knack of it.
3 Cut the top layer into strips three or four inches ($7\frac{1}{2}$ or 10 cm) wide.
4 Spread the filling on the uncut bottom layer, then lay the strips on this and use them as a guide to cut through the bottom layer.
5 Finish and decorate the strips according to the original recipe.

For GÂTEAU SLICES cut each strip into several small, oblong pieces before finishing and decorating.

Gâteau Saint Honoré *page 94*

Linzer Torte *page 88*   Gâteau Edouard *page 83*

Millefeuille Gâteau *page 84*

late cream and place in refrigerator for about 20 minutes.

3 Add the chopped pineapple to some of the plain whipped cream and spread this nice solid mixture on the gâteau, bringing it level with the cone of chocolate cream.

4 Place the other round of the sandwich sponge on top of all this and cover with the remaining whipped cream.

5 Dust the top of the cake lightly with cocoa powder and mark it into portions (8 or 12 depending on how generous you are feeling) and then put a blob of cream and one or two pieces of pineapple on every portion. Decorate the sides with chocolate vermicelli as described on page 119.

Gâteau La Marquise

I don't know who the marquise was to whom this delightful confection was dedicated but I imagine her as cultivated, rich, dedicatedly fun loving and frequently unfaithful to the marquis – possibly with a pastry cook!

½ oz (15 g) powdered gelatine
a little hot water
4 egg yolks
1 teaspoon coffee powder
2 oz (60 g) caster sugar
¾ pint (4.5 dl) milk
10 sponge fingers
2 tablespoons rum
¼ pint (1.5 dl) double cream
2 oz (60 g) sieved, red jam ⎫
½ pint (3 dl) double cream ⎬ for topping
⎭

8″ (20 cm) sponge tin – 10″ (25 cm) serving dish – 2 mixing bowls – 2 cups or small bowls – 2 pint (1 litre) saucepan – wooden spoon – coarse sieve – savoy bag, rosette pipe – greaseproof paper piping bag – palette knife – whisk – soup plate

1 Put about three tablespoons of hot water into a cup, sprinkle the gelatine over the surface and leave to soak for 5–7 minutes. (Keep this warm to prevent it setting before use.)

2 Beat together the egg yolks, coffee and sugar until creamy in texture.

3 Heat the milk but DO NOT LET IT BOIL, then pour it into the egg mixture, stirring gently but thoroughly.

4 Strain this mixture, through a coarse sieve, back into the saucepan.

5 Add the gelatine and water and stir steadily over a low heat until the gelatine is completely dissolved, about 2 or 3 minutes.

6 Pour the mixture back into the bowl and leave in a cool (not cold) place until the mixture has cooled and is beginning to thicken.

7 While the mixture is cooling, soak the sponge fingers in the rum. This is best done in the soup plate.

8 Whisk the $\frac{1}{4}$ pint (1.5 dl) of double cream until it is thick and fold it into the now thickened egg mixture.

9 Lightly moisten the inside of the sponge tin.

10 Pour half the mixture into the sponge tin.

11 Arrange the soaked sponge fingers on this mixture like the spokes of a wheel and pour the remainder of the mixture on top.

12 Put this into the refrigerator for about 1 hour.

13 Just before it is time to remove the chilled cake from the refrigerator, whip the cream for the topping.

14 Remove the cake from the refrigerator, easing the sides gently from the tin – you can dip the base of the tin into hot water for a few seconds if necessary – and carefully turn out on to the serving dish.

15 Put almost half the whipped cream into the savoy bag, fitted with the rosette pipe.

16 Spread the remainder of the whipped cream evenly and smoothly over the top and sides of the cake with the palette knife.

17 Pipe circlets of whipped cream round the top outside edge of the cake.

18 Put the sieved red jam into the paper piping bag and pipe blobs of jam into the centre of every circlet of whipped cream.

19 Keep chilled until ready to serve.

Malakoff Torte

Malakoff is an unremarkable suburb of Paris but, if this recipe is anything to go by, the people who live there have a fine taste in cakes!

8 oz (230 g) butter
6 oz (175 g) caster sugar
1 egg yolk
1 oz (30 g) coffee powder
2 oz (60 g) candied peel, finely chopped
1 oz (30 g) walnuts, finely chopped
2 oz (60 g) ground almonds
¼ pint (1.5 dl) rum
¼ pint (1.5 dl) water
36 sponge fingers
2 oz (60 g) unsweetened chocolate
¼ pint (1.5 dl) double cream
⅛ pint (0.75 dl) milk

8″ (20 cm) cake tin with loose bottom – baking tray – 2 bowls – whisk – tablespoon – grinder – sharp knife – spatula – measuring jug – wooden spoon – saucepan – palette knife – flat dish – savoy bag and tube – greaseproof paper and foil

1 Line the base and sides of the cake tin with greaseproof paper.
2 Put the butter and sugar into one of the bowls and cream together until it is pale, the sugar should still be slightly gritty.
3 Beat the egg yolk and add to the butter and sugar mixture, then add the coffee and fold in the candied peel and chopped mixed nuts.
4 Blend together the rum and water and pour into a flat dish.
5 Crumple some foil and shape into a collar to fit inside the base of the cake tin, but leave a gap between the tin and the foil.
6 Moisten some of the biscuits or fingers in the dish of rum for a few seconds but do not allow them to soften.
7 Place the soaked biscuits around the tin in the gap between the foil and the sides of the tin.
8 Remove the foil very carefully from the tin, easing it up the sides, leaving the biscuits remaining in position.
9 Line the base of the tin with some more of the soaked biscuits carefully one at a time and spread with half the coffee mixture.

10 Whip the cream until it is thick, then spoon some on to the coffee mixture, spreading evenly with the spatula.

11 Put some soaked biscuits over the cream, then the rest of the coffee mixture and the remaining cream, finally adding the remaining soaked biscuits on top of the cream.

12 Cut off the tops of the biscuits which extend above the cake.

13 Put into the refrigerator for at least 1 hour before serving.

Boszorkanyhab or Witches' Cream

This witches' brew isn't quite as exotic as the one you will find in Macbeth but, I think you'll agree, it's a good deal nicer!

2 lb (960 g) cooking apples
2 or 3 egg whites
8 oz (230 g) caster sugar
6 oz (175 g) sliced fresh fruit
½ pint (3 dl) whipped cream
a little lemon juice

glass dish – sieve – 2 bowls – whisk

1 Bake the apples in the pre-set oven (350°F/175°C/Gas 4) until they are very soft then remove from the oven and peel, skin and core them.

2 Pass the apples through a sieve and leave to get cold.

3 Whip the whites of the eggs and add the sieved apple gradually beating to a very stiff snow.

4 Add the sugar and lemon juice to the mixture and mix well together.

5 Pour the mixture into the glass dish and decorate the top with slices of fresh fruit and whipped cream.

6 Put into the refrigerator for at least 1 hour before serving.

Coffee Brandy Gâteau

A lovely summer's evening in the country; dinner is being eaten on the terrace, on the patio or simply

6 oz (175 g) butter
6 oz (175 g) caster sugar
3 large eggs
1 oz (30 g) coffee powder
⅛ pint (0.75 dl) brandy
12 sponge fingers

on the lawn. The first course was tantalisingly gossamer, the meat course was the subtlest blend of flavours served with a perfectly balanced selection of vegetables. The Venus or Adonis by your side really seems interested. Now a coffee brandy gâteau is served. 'Tis such stuff that dreams are made of.

¼ pint (1.5 dl) whipped cream
chopped walnuts for decoration

8″ (20 cm) loose bottom cake tin, lined with non-stick paper – 2 bowls – whisk – sharp knife – spatula – icing bag and nozzle – plate – palette knife

1 Put the butter and sugar into one of the bowls and beat together until light and fluffy, taking care not to over beat but at the same time making sure that the sugar is not gritty.
2 Add the eggs one at a time and beat gently after each addition.
3 Add the instant coffee and brandy to the mixture and mix well.
4 Cut the sponge fingers in half lengthwise and place 8 pieces in the base of the cake tin. Pour half the coffee mixture over these, then add a further 8 pieces, and pour the remaining coffee mixture on top of these.
5 Arrange the remaining pieces of sponge on top of the coffee mixture and press down well. Now cover the tin with a plate and place a weight on top of it.
6 Put the tin in the refrigerator for about 3 hours by which time the cake should be set.
7 Remove from the refrigerator and run a round bladed knife or a palette knife around the edge of the tin to loosen the cake.
8 Turn the gâteau out on to a plate and spread some of the whipped cream evenly on the top.
9 To decorate, pipe the remaining whipped cream around the top of the gâteau and place the chopped walnuts in the centre.

Special Occasion Cakes

It took a lot of heart-searching before I could bring myself to put these recipes into a separate section. If they are good enough to be used for special occasions then they are too good to be used only once or twice a year. So why not have lots more special occasions in your year like, 'It is exactly sixty-seven days since Uncle Clarence stayed sober till half-past seven.' What a wonderful excuse for a special cake – if you really need an excuse.

Light Fruit Birthday Cake

Of course, this cake need not be limited to birthdays. I believe it was Humpty Dumpty in Alice Through the Looking Glass *who pronounced on un-birthday presents so why not un-birthday cakes! Anyway, let me give you a tip which should stop it or any other fruit cake going dry too quickly: just add a little pure glycerine to the mix – a teaspoon or so. It is tasteless and so won't affect the flavour of your cake. Why haven't I used it here! Well some people think that it's cheating. But who's to know!*

OVEN TEMPERATURE:
350°F/180°C/GAS 4

4 oz (115 g) butter
4 oz (115 g) soft brown sugar
1½ oz (45 g) golden syrup
2 eggs
6 oz (175 g) plain flour
1 level teaspoon baking powder
large pinch of salt
1 level teaspoon mixed spice
11 oz (315 g) sultanas, currants, glacé cherries, angelica and other dried fruits mixed together
2 oz (60 g) candied peel
a little milk

7" (20 cm) cake tin, lined – whisk – sieve – 2 bowls – spatula

1 Toss the dried fruit in a little flour to prevent the fruit sticking together.
2 Sift together the flour, salt, baking powder and mixed spice.
3 In one bowl cream together the butter, sugar and syrup being very careful to ensure that while all these ingredients are thoroughly blended, the butter does not separate.
4 In the other bowl whisk the eggs.

5 Add the whisked eggs and the flour mixture alternately (a spoonful of egg, a bit of flour, more egg, more flour, etc.) to the creamed fat, beating as these are added.

6 Gently stir in the mixed fruit.

7 If the mixture begins to get hard and tacky, add a little milk very slowly, making sure that only just enough milk is added to make the mix 'workable'. If it becomes too soft all the fruit will sink to the bottom.

8 Put the mixture into the lined cake tin, spreading it so that there are no bubbles and so that it is slightly lower in the centre than at the sides – it is the centre of the cake that rises most and you will want it as flat as possible to decorate.

9 Put it into the pre-heated oven for the first half hour. Reduce the heat to 300°F/150°C Gas 1–2 and bake for a further 2–2½ hours until it is firm and light brown in colour.

10 Remove from cake tin and leave to cool on a rack.

For decorating, see pages 122–5.

Wedding Cake

Even in this allegedly enlightened and sophisticated age most people have only one wedding in their lives and the wedding day is still very much the bride's day – or it is if only her mother will allow it! Unfeeling cynics sometimes suggest that the groom is there only to make up numbers . . . Be that as it may, it is a very important day on which friends and seldom seen relatives assemble from far and near.

After the bride's father has proposed the toast to the bride and groom, after the groom has muttered and stuttered his reply and said 'my wife and I' for the first

These ingredients will make a two-tier cake weighing about 10 lb (4.5 kg).

8 oz (230 g) marzipan and enough white of egg to soften it
8 oz (230 g) margarine
8 oz (230 g) butter
1 lb (460 g) demerara sugar
2 oz (60 g) caramelised sugar*
8 large eggs
1 lb 2 oz (520 g) plain flour
4 lb (1.8 kg) currants
1 lb (460 g) sultanas
4 oz (115 g) chopped mixed peel
8 oz (230 g) glacé cherries
¼ pint (1.4 dl) brandy

the proportions are variable according to taste but the total should stay about 5 lb 12 oz (2.6 kg)

time, after 'Uncle Clarence' has made a speech in questionable taste, after the best man has read all those hilarious, stereotyped telegrams and proposed the toast of the bridesmaids then, at last, we come to the high spot of the reception. 'Ladies and Gentlemen, the bride and groom are about to cut the cake.' Every eye in the room is on that cake – even Uncle Clarence's though he has difficulty in focusing! You made that cake. You are proud of it. And so you should be. You made it carefully and lovingly and if a tear drop or two fell into the mixing, however salty your tears, they will have added to the sweetness.

The top tier can be put into an air tight tin and used, in due course, as a Christening cake; but not yet, not just yet.

OVEN TEMPERATURE:
290°F/145°C/GAS $\frac{1}{2}$–1

very large bowl – strong whisk – spatula – palette knife – pointed knife or skewer – cake tin(s) to size required, greased – greaseproof paper

1 Soften the marzipan with a little white of egg.
2 Cream this together with the margarine, butter and demerara sugar until the mixture is smooth and light.
3 Colour it with the caramel, mix this well in until the colour is even.
4 Beat the eggs in one at a time until the mixture is very light, almost fluffy in texture.
5 Sieve the flour into the mixture and fold it in – do not over work the mixture at this point or it will not hold the fruit which will all sink to the bottom.
6 Add the fruit and blend it in thoroughly but gently.
7 Put the mixture into the cake tin(s) and smooth the top with the palette knife.
8 Bake for about 1 hour 10 minutes (larger cakes will take a bit longer).
9 Turn the cake(s) out of the tin(s) to cool.
10 When the cake(s) are completely cooled, pierce the underside several times with a pointed knife or skewer and pour the brandy on slowly so that it soaks into the cake.
11 Wrap the cake(s) in greaseproof paper and store in a cool, dry place (not the refrigerator) for not less than 48 hours before decorating.

* Caramelising sugar is not quite as simple as it seems. To make about 1 lb 8 oz (690 g) see the recipe that follows. Otherwise, buy a few caramel or butterscotch sweets and melt them down slowly in a little water and allow the mixture to darken a little. Use an old saucepan for this.

For the CARAMEL:
6 oz (175 g) butter
6 oz (175 g) condensed milk
8 oz (230 g) granulated sugar
4 oz (115 g) demerara sugar
$\frac{1}{4}$ pint (1.25 dl) water
6 oz (175 g) dextrose

small saucepan – large, old, thick based saucepan – spatula – sugar thermometer – metal tray – sharp knife

1 Mix the butter and condensed milk in the small saucepan over a very low heat.
2 Put the sugars, dextrose and water into the large saucepan and bring to the boil (280°F–140°C) stirring continuously.
3 Remove from the heat and slowly and steadily stir in the butter-milk mixture.
4 Return to a medium heat and continue to cook slowly until 'hard crack'* is reached.
5 If the caramel is to be added to a cake mix, now is the time to add it. Otherwise, pour into a metal tray, lightly greased, and allow to cool.
6 When almost cool, cut into convenient sizes using firm, brisk strokes of the knife.

* The toffee will snap when a little is cooled in a cup of cold water.

Christmas Cake

When I was a little boy my father used to tell me wonderful stories which he made up as he went along – at least that is what he led me to believe. They were serials and every instalment was more enchanting than the last. Among the best of these was 'The Summer Santa Claus'. It was probably the idea of an extra lot of Christmas presents and Christmas fare that appealed to me. But then, why not!

OVEN TEMPERATURE:
335°F/170°C/GAS 3–4

8 oz (230 g) butter
8 oz (230 g) soft brown sugar
1 level teaspoon black treacle
4 eggs
10 oz (285 g) plain flour
1 level teaspoon baking powder
¼ teaspoon salt
1 teaspoon coffee powder
1 level teaspoon mixed spice
½ level teaspoon ground ginger
a few drops vanilla essence
1 generous tot of rum
1 good teaspoon almond oil
a little lemon juice
8 oz (230 g) currants
8 oz (230 g) sultanas
3 oz (85 g) chopped, mixed peel
8 oz (230 g) raisins
3–4 oz (85–115 g) blanched, chopped almonds
a little rum or brandy for final touch

8" (20 cm) cake tin, lined – sieve – whisk – spatula – 2 bowls

1 Toss the dried fruit in a little flour to prevent the fruit sticking together.
2 Sift together the flour, baking powder, salt, instant coffee powder and spices.
3 In one bowl cream together the butter, sugar and treacle until it is thoroughly blended and a creamy texture.
4 In the other bowl beat the eggs well.
5 Add a little of the beaten egg to the creamed butter and beat well together.
6 Add flour and egg alternately until half of both flour and egg has been used, beating steadily all the time.
7 Add the remainder of the egg slowly and steadily, beating continuously.
8 Add the vanilla essence, rum, lemon juice and almond oil and beat in thoroughly.
9 Slowly mix in the remainder of the flour making sure the flour is completely mixed in.
10 Add the fruits and nuts, increasing the mixing speed slightly. Take care not to break up the fruits and also not to over mix as this will make the fruit sink to the bottom of the cake.
11 Put the mixture into the lined cake tin, spreading evenly to avoid bubbles.
12 Place in the centre of the oven and bake at set temperature for 1 hour. Reduce temperature to 290°F (145°C) Gas $\frac{1}{2}$–1 and bake for about another 2 hours until the cake is well set, risen and of a good even colour.
13 Remove from oven and allow to cool on a rack.
14 Place in an air-tight tin to store. You may wish to remove the top 'skin' and sprinkle the cake liberally with rum or brandy before storing.

For decoration see pages 122–5.

Plum Cake

This, of course, was the original Christmas cake (or was it!). It is rich, it is filling, it is delicious and it tastes just as good in July (if the weather isn't too hot) as it does in December.

OVEN TEMPERATURE:
335°F/170°C/GAS 3–4

8 oz (230 g) butter
8 oz (230 g) caster sugar
4 eggs
½ teaspoon almond oil
grated rind of 1 lemon
10 oz (285 g) plain flour
¼ teaspoon salt
3 or 4 oz (85 or 115 g) mixed peel
16 oz (460 g) glacé cherries, raisins, currants, prunes cut in quarters, and the like
2 oz (60 g) ground almonds
a very generous tot of brandy

8" (20 cm) cake tin, lined – 2 bowls – sieve – whisk – grater – pointed knife – greaseproof paper or waxed paper or air-tight cake tin

1 Toss the dried fruit in a little flour to prevent the fruit from sticking together.
2 Sift the flour and salt together.
3 Cream together the butter and sugar until white and fluffy, making sure that the butter does not separate.
4 Beat the eggs thoroughly.
5 Add the beaten eggs to the creamed butter a little at a time. See that the eggs are evenly beaten in but do not over beat.
6 Add both the almond oil and lemon rind and mix in slowly but thoroughly.
7 Fold in about a quarter of the flour. This is to make the mixture firm enough to hold the fruit.
8 Stir in the floured fruit and the ground almonds, ensuring that they are evenly spread throughout the mixture but taking care not to break the fruit up.
9 Fold in the remainder of the flour.
10 Put the mixture into the lined cake tin.
11 Place the tin near the top of the pre-set oven and bake for half an hour.
12 Reduce the heat to 310°F (155°C) Gas 2–3 and continue to bake for another 2–2½ hours.
13 When baked, remove the cake from the tin and allow it to cool, preferably on a rack.

14 Make several deep cuts in the bottom of the cake with a pointed knife and pour in the brandy which will penetrate the cake. Do not be tempted to add the brandy before baking as it will simply evaporate.

15 Wrap the cake in the greaseproof or waxed paper or put it into the air-tight tin and store in a cool, dry place for two or three weeks.

Log Cake

This is that something extra you will be glad to have when unexpected callers arrive on Boxing Day.

OVEN TEMPERATURE:
410°F/210°C/GAS 6–7

CAKE
6 eggs
2 oz (60 g) caster sugar
2 oz (60 g) plain flour
FILLING
2 oz (60 g) butter
a little milk
5 oz (145 g) grated walnuts
a little grated lemon peel
DECORATION
2 oz (60 g) butter
2 oz (60 g) caster sugar
1 egg yolk
3 oz (85 g) melted chocolate

baking tray, greased – 3 bowls – whisk – spatula – palette knife – grater – cooling rack

CAKE
1 Separate the egg whites and yolks into two of the bowls.
2 Add the sugar and flour to the egg yolks and mix well together.
3 Whisk the egg whites until they are stiff and firm.
4 Fold the stiffly beaten egg whites into the mixture carefully and lightly.
5 Pour the mixture into the prepared baking tray.
6 Bake in the pre-set oven for 12–20 minutes.
7 Remove from the oven, place on the cooling rack and allow to cool.

FILLING

1 Put the softened butter and milk into a bowl and gently mix together.
2 Add the grated walnuts and lemon peel.
3 Spread the butter filling over the cake evenly with the palette knife, then roll it up like a swiss roll (see page 44.)

DECORATION

1 Mix the butter, sugar and egg yolk together to form a smooth consistency, then add the melted chocolate and mix well but lightly together.
2 Cover the log cake with this mixture and allow to set.
3 Pieces of walnuts may be added to the top of the cake as a finishing touch.

Mince Pies

Here are two recipes for mince pies, one with short pastry and one with puff pastry. Personally, I prefer the first. Here also is a recipe for mincemeat which can be varied according to taste. As long as you can store mincemeat properly (like jam) you can't make it too early. I know you can also buy it ready made, but that is not what we are about.

Mincemeat

8 oz (230 g) cooking apples
8 oz (230 g) currants
8 oz (230 g) raisins
8 oz (230 g) sultanas
4 oz (115 g) chopped mixed peel
4 oz (115 g) chopped walnuts
8 oz (230 g) shredded suet
1 lb (460 g) demerara sugar
1 oz (30 g) mixed spice
$\frac{1}{4}$ pint (1.5 dl) brandy or rum

large bowl – cloth – strong wooden spoon – apple peeler – mincer – 6 × 1 lb (460 g) jars or 12 × 8 oz (230 g) jars – greaseproof paper – elastic bands or string

1 Peel, core and chop the apples.
2 Wash and mince the dried fruit.
3 Mix the chopped apple, minced fruit and chopped nuts in the bowl.
4 Blend in the shredded suet, sugar and spice.
5 Add and stir in the brandy or rum.
6 Cover the bowl and leave to stand for at least 48 hours.
7 Stir the mixture well.

8 Put the mixture into jars and cover the tops with greaseproof paper held on with elastic bands or string.

9 Store for at least a month before using.

Mince Pies (Short Pastry)

OVEN TEMPERATURE:
450°F/230°C/GAS 8

2 lb (920 g) short pastry (see page 133)
6 lb (2.75 kg) mincemeat (see page 109)
a little caster sugar and flour for dusting
cold water

rolling pin – pastry board – sharp knife or skewer – cutter – tablespoon – tart cases, greased – baking trays

1 Roll out a little more than half the pastry to less than $\frac{1}{4}$" (0.5 cm) thick on a floured pastry board.

2 Roll out the remaining pastry a bit thinner.

3 Cut both into discs the right size for your tart cases, keeping the thick and thin separate.

4 Line every tart case with one of the thicker discs, press them well in but take care not to pierce the paste.

5 Fill up with mincemeat softened with a little water if necessary.

6 Put a thin disc over the mincemeat and seal the base and top together.

7 Sprinkle caster sugar over the pies.

8 Pierce a hole in the top of each one.

9 Bake in the pre-set oven for about 20 minutes.

Mince Pies (Puff Pastry)

OVEN TEMPERATURE:
475°F/250°C/GAS 9

2 lb (920 g) puff pastry (see page 134)
6 lb (2.75 kg) mincemeat (see page 109)
a little caster sugar and flour for dusting
cold water

rolling pin – pastry board – pointed knife or skewer – pastry brush – tablespoon – 2" cutter – 2 or 3 baking trays, greased

1 Roll out a little more than half the puff pastry

to a little less than $\frac{1}{4}''$ (0.5 cm) thick on a floured pastry board.

2 Roll out the remaining pastry a bit thinner.

3 Cut both with the cutter into 2" discs, keeping the thick and thin separate.

4 Lay out the thicker discs on the baking trays.

5 Put a generous spoonful of mincemeat into the centre of every disc.

6 Dampen the visible outer ring of every disc with water.

7 Place a thin disc over the mincemeat and press down the edges to seal. (The blunt side of a smaller cutter or an old coffee cup may be useful for this.)

8 Sprinkle all the pies with caster sugar.

9 Pierce a hole in the top of every pie.

10 Bake in the pre-set oven for about 20 minutes.

January Cake or Twelfth Night Cake

A good way to wind up the ballyhoo of Christmas is with a little party on Twelfth Night, the official end of the 'festive season'. Why not serve this cake on that occasion! And at other times too.

OVEN TEMPERATURE:
335°F/170°C/GAS 3–4

12 oz (345 g) plain flour
$\frac{1}{4}$ teaspoon salt
6 oz (175g) butter
3 oz (85 g) soft brown sugar
3 eggs
1 level teaspoon baking powder
$\frac{1}{2}$ gill (0.75 dl) milk
2 oz (60 g) treacle
4 oz (115 g) currants
4 oz (115 g) sultanas
4 oz (115 g) mixed peel
$\frac{1}{2}$ teaspoon ground cinnamon
$\frac{1}{2}$ teaspoon mixed spice

sieve – 2 bowls – whisk – spatula – 7" (20 cm) cake tin, lined

1 Toss the dried fruit in a little flour to prevent the fruit from sticking together.

2 Sift together the flour and salt. Do not add the baking powder yet.

3 Cream together the butter and the sugar until it is white and fluffy, taking care that the butter does not separate.

4 Add the eggs one at a time and beat in thoroughly. Blend every egg in well before adding the next.

5 Dissolve the baking powder in a little milk and add this to the mixture. You may find it helpful to warm the milk slightly first.

6 Pour in the treacle slowly and steadily, beating gently all the while. (It may be helpful to warm it first so that it pours more easily.) Continue beating until the treacle is completely absorbed in the mixture.

7 Very gently fold in about a quarter of the flour. This makes the mixture firm enough to hold the fruit.

8 Stir in the fruit and the ground cinnamon and the mixed spice. Make sure that this is evenly spread through the mixture, but avoid breaking up the fruit.

9 Fold in the remainder of the flour and salt mixture, beating slowly until the mixture is of an even consistency.

10 Bake in the centre of the oven for 2–2½ hours.

11 Remove from cake tin and allow to cool.

February Cake or Valentine's Cake

Valentine's Day may be cause for celebration. If it is not, make this cake some other winter's day.

OVEN TEMPERATURE:
350°F/180°C/GAS 4

3 oz (85 g) butter
3 oz (85 g) caster sugar
grated rind of 1 lemon or 1 orange, or a mixture of both
2 eggs
4 oz (115 g) plain flour
¼ oz (8 g) baking powder
a pinch of salt

7" (20 cm) cake tin or heart-shaped baking tin – bowl – grater – sieve – whisk

1 Grate the orange and/or lemon peel.

2 Sift together the flour, salt and baking powder.

3 Cream the butter and sugar until it is white and fluffy, taking care that the butter does not separate.

4 Beat in the grated peel.

Wedding Cake *page 103*

Cottage Loaf *page 150*

Cheese Pastry Biscuits *page 140*   Floris Bread *page 151*

Savoury Florentines *page 140*   Cheese Straws *page 139*

5 Add the eggs one at a time. Make sure the first egg is well mixed in before adding the second.

6 Fold in the flour and beat steadily, ensuring the mixture is of an even consistency.

7 Put the mixture into the cake tin; either the 7″ (20 cm) or the heart-shaped one, whichever you have chosen.

8 Bake in the centre of the oven for between 45 minutes and 1 hour.

9 Eat a piece about half an hour before bedtime and dream of the one you love. (For the most romantic results, the heart-shaped tin is recommended!)

Simnel Cake

There are a number of versions of how this cake originated. I like to think it was dreamed up by poor Lambert Simnel while he served out his time as a cook in King Henry's kitchens after the fiasco of his attempt on the throne itself . . .

OVEN TEMPERATURE:
300°F/150°C/GAS 1–2

1 lb (460 g) ready made almond paste
8 oz (230 g) plain flour
a pinch of salt
½ teaspoon of grated nutmeg
¼ teaspoon of powdered cinnamon
8 oz (230 g) currants
4 oz (115 g) sultanas
3 oz (85 g) mixed peel, chopped
4 oz (115 g) glacé cherries
6 oz (175 g) butter
6 oz (175 g) caster sugar
3 eggs
1 egg white
milk to mix, if required

7″ (20 cm) cake tin, round, greased and lined – rolling pin – 4 bowls – sieve – spatula – sharp knife – cutter – pastry brush – pastry board – cooling rack

1 Place one third of the almond paste on the pastry board and roll out to a round, cut the round slightly smaller than the cake tin and leave for the present.

2 In one of the bowls mix together the sifted flour, salt and spices.

3 In the second bowl mix the washed fruit together.

4 In the third bowl put the butter and sugar and cream them together until pale and fluffy, add the eggs one at a time and beat into the mixture.

5 Fold the flour into the mixture carefully, adding if necessary a drop of milk until the mixture has a dropping consistency, then fold in the mixed washed fruit and stir the ingredients well but gently together.

6 Put half the mixture into the cake tin and place the round of almond paste on the top of the mixture.

7 Put the remaining mixture on top of the round of almond paste, making sure to spread it evenly.

8 Bake in the pre-set oven for $2\frac{1}{2}$–3 hours, or until it is a rich brown colour and firm to touch.

9 Remove from the oven and turn out on to the cooling rack.

10 While the cake is cooling, using the remaining almond paste make a round to fit the top of the cake and allow enough over to shape eleven small balls.

11 When the cake is cold brush the top with a little egg white and place the paste round on top of it, smoothing it gently with the rolling pin, then pinch the edges of the paste into scallops with the tips of the finger and thumb.

12 Using a sharp knife score the surface of the cake into a lattice pattern, brush this with a little of the egg white and arrange the almond balls on the top of the cake, brushing these too with a little egg white.

13 Place the cake under a moderate grill until it is a light golden brown colour and allow to cool.

Hot Cross Buns

The Greeks made cakes with 'horns' on them to offer to Apollo, Diana and Hecate on their name days. These cakes were supposed never to go mouldy. The original hot cross buns were supposed to be made from dough kneaded for the Host and were marked with a cross partly for that reason and partly to commemorate the first Good Friday. The notion that they won't go mouldy still persists in some homes where every year one bun is hung up 'to ward off evil' and remains until it is replaced the following Easter.

OVEN TEMPERATURE:
425°F/220°C/GAS 7

1 oz (30 g) yeast
½ pint (2.75 dl) milk
3 oz (85 g) caster sugar
1 lb (460 g) plain flour
½ oz (15 g) salt
½ oz (15 g) cinnamon ⎫ or according to
½ oz (15 g) nutmeg ⎬ taste
1 oz (30 g) mixed spice ⎭
3 oz (85 g) butter
2 eggs
4 oz (115 g) currants
1 oz (30 g) chopped peel
1 egg ⎫
¼ pint (1.5 dl) milk ⎬ for glazing
2 oz (60 g) caster sugar ⎭

small bowl – large bowl – pastry board – knife – pastry brush – fork – baking sheet(s), greased

1 In the small bowl dissolve the yeast in the milk with a little of the sugar.
2 Sieve the flour, salt and spice together into the large bowl.
3 Make a well in the flour and put in the dissolved yeast, the remainder of the sugar and the butter and mix these together thoroughly.
4 Add the eggs one at a time and work the dough until smooth and fine.
5 Add the currants and chopped peel and knead until it no longer sticks to your hands and the dough looks and feels like satin.
6 Cover the bowl with a cloth and put it in a warm place to rise for about an hour.
7 'Knock it back' and knead it again lightly, then cover with a cloth and allow to rise for about half an hour.
8 Put the dough on to a floured pastry board, cut it into pieces about 1 oz (30 g) in weight.
9 Mould the pieces into balls by rolling them on the board under the palms of your hands.
10 Place the buns on the baking sheets and again allow them to rise in a warm place for about 15 minutes.
11 While they are rising for the last time, mix

the egg, milk and sugar together with the fork in the small bowl, which you have washed.
12 Brush the buns with this glaze.
13 Lightly cut a cross on every bun or place crosses on them as described below.
14 Bake in the pre-set oven for about 15 minutes.

For the CROSSES:
4 oz (115 g) plain flour
½ oz (15 g) pastry margarine
¼ pint (1.5 dl) water

bowl – pastry board – rolling pin – knife

1 Sieve the flour.
2 Add the fat and water and mix well together.
3 Put the paste on to a floured board and roll out as thin as it will go. You will need to keep the rolling pin dusted with flour to do this.
4 Cut the paste into thin strips and these strips into lengths of about 1½″ (4 cm).
5 Place two of these short strips in the shape of a cross on every bun after the bun has been glazed.
6 Bake as described.

Easter Buns

Everyone has hot cross buns at Easter time – so let's just be a little different.

OVEN TEMPERATURE:
425°F/220°C/GAS 7

3 eggs
a little milk as required
½ oz (15 g) yeast
1 lb (460 g) plain flour
4 oz (115 g) butter
4 oz (115 g) caster sugar
a pinch of salt
1 egg yolk
a little caster sugar } for glazing

2 bowls – saucepan – whisk – pastry board – rolling pin – pastry brush – baking tray

1 In one of the bowls beat the eggs lightly.
2 Warm the milk in the saucepan.
3 Pour the milk into the second bowl and mix in the yeast and leave it to rise for about 15 minutes.

4 Add and mix in the flour, salt, butter and sugar, cover with a cloth and let it rise again for about 20 minutes.

5 Mix in the beaten eggs, a little at a time, until the mixture is well blended together. Leave to rise again, this time for about 30 minutes.

6 Put the mixture on to a floured pastry board and roll it out to a thickness of $\frac{1}{4}''$ (0.5 cm).

7 *Either* cut this with a 4″ (10 cm) cutter *or* cut into strips about 6″ (15 cm) long and $\frac{1}{2}''$ (1 cm) wide. Plait two of these together and form them into a circle.

8 Cover them again with a cloth and leave to rise yet again for about 30 minutes.

9 When the dough has risen sufficiently, brush the strips or buns with a little egg yolk mixed with sugar, then leave to rise again.

10 Finally, before placing the dough pieces on to the baking sheet or tray, brush again with the egg yolk mixture and bake in the oven.

11 As a finishing touch you may care to decorate with hard boiled eggs placed in the centre of the ring-shaped buns.

Decorating

This is the most difficult part of the book for me to write. It is almost impossible to describe the process of decorating a cake. I wish I could be with you in the kitchen. But even then so much would depend on your artistic ability. Some lucky people have a natural talent for decorating. Some will always be fumblers. Let me assume here, however, that you have the dexterity and the artistic imagination that each of us would like to be blessed with . . .

Decorating Gâteaux

Gâteaux can be finished with cream, butter cream, fondant icing or chocolate. Flaked and crushed nuts, cake crumbs and chocolate vermicelli are also frequently used as are all sorts of glazed fruits, nuts, chocolate pieces, jam, jelly and marzipan.

To finish a gâteau with cream or butter cream, first make sure that your cream is whisked to a firm but workable consistency. Now, hold the cake on the tips of the fingers of your left hand so that you can rotate it slowly and steadily. With your other hand load a palette knife with some cream (the same flavour as the sponge or filling of the gâteau or a carefully selected contrasting flavour) and holding the palette knife at a slight angle to the side of the gâteau, rotate the gâteau so that you 'butter' the side with the cream. The thickness of this is partly a matter of taste but largely one of appearance. If it is too thin the sponge will show through, if it is too thick it will be inclined to slide to the bottom.

Now put the gâteau on your turntable (if you have no turntable, then on a low surface) and spread cream over the top of it. Smooth this over either by holding the palette knife at a slight angle to the surface and turning the turntable or by taking the palette knife or other straight edge, larger than the diameter of the gâteau, and holding it in both hands, drawing it gently and steadily across the top. Remove any surplus from the top edge by holding the palette knife very lightly at an angle of about 45° to the edge and turning the gâteau either on the turntable or as described earlier.

Now all sorts of things are possible. The easiest is to produce a 'snow' effect by tapping the creamed surface lightly with the flat of the palette knife. Next easiest is to draw a fork or a serrated edge around the side and over the top in a straight or wavy motion. (Many pastry cooks have a plastic or metal scraper with a serrated edge for this purpose.)

The edge can be covered with crushed (not ground) nuts, cake crumbs or chocolate vermicelli by rotating the cake as described previously, while applying a small handful of the nuts or whatever to the sides of the gâteau with your free hand.

The top of the gâteau can be decorated by piping a design around the edge, in the centre, over the whole surface or any combination of these. To do this fit a tube of your choice – the star tube is very effective – to your savoy bag and holding the top of it with your right hand and the tube with the left (vice versa if you are left handed) squeeze gently but steadily with the top hand and guide with both. The tip of the tube should be about $\frac{1}{4}$" to $\frac{1}{2}$" ($1-1\frac{1}{2}$ cm) from the surface being decorated.

With a number of tubes – the more the merrier – an almost infinite number of effects can be achieved. I suggest that you sacrifice a small amount of butter cream and experiment on a metal or laminated plastic surface. After every attempt you can scrape the butter cream off the surface and start again. You will find that interesting results can be obtained by slight variations in the pressure, altering the angle at which you are holding the piping bag, slight (or not so slight), movements of the lower hand and so on. One popular top edging, for example, is scalloping.

To get this effect use a star tube, move the tube away from you a fraction and then come back over that spot reducing the pressure by the top hand steadily to none. Every scallop should be about $\frac{1}{2}$" (1.5 cm) long, but this too is infinitely variable.

To fondant ice a gâteau prepare your fondant (see page 130) then put your gâteau on a wire rack which is standing on a tray or board and simply pour the warm fondant over the gâteau spreading it evenly over the top and sides with a palette knife. With many gâteaux it will help to cover it first with a little jam glaze – strained jam, mixed with an equal quantity of water and heated and stirred till it is well mixed. But please avoid boiling it. This will help the fondant to stick to the gâteau. Allow the fondant to set for a few moments then trim any surplus from the bottom edge. You may prefer to have fondant only on the top and to cover the sides with crushed nuts, cake crumbs or chocolate vermicelli. I have seen gâteaux with fondant icing on the top and buttercream on the sides but I don't like the idea. Further decoration is now possible with piping – a fine, plain tube is needed here because, as fondant has to be molten, you can only use a little at a time. You may prefer to make your own piping bag out of greaseproof paper as follows:

1 Cut a perfect square of greaseproof paper.
2 Cut this into two triangles.
3 Lay it on a table the long edge nearest to you. Put the tip of a finger on the centre of this edge and roll the left point (right if you are left handed) towards the top point.
4 Hold the top with one hand and adjust the bottom with the other so that it makes a fine point.
5 Roll the other point round the back of the bag.
6 Fold the loose ends and tuck them in to fasten securely.
7 With very sharp scissors cut a little off the tip of the bag to make a hole of the thickness you require or to allow a piping tube to be usable. These paper bags can be used without a tube.

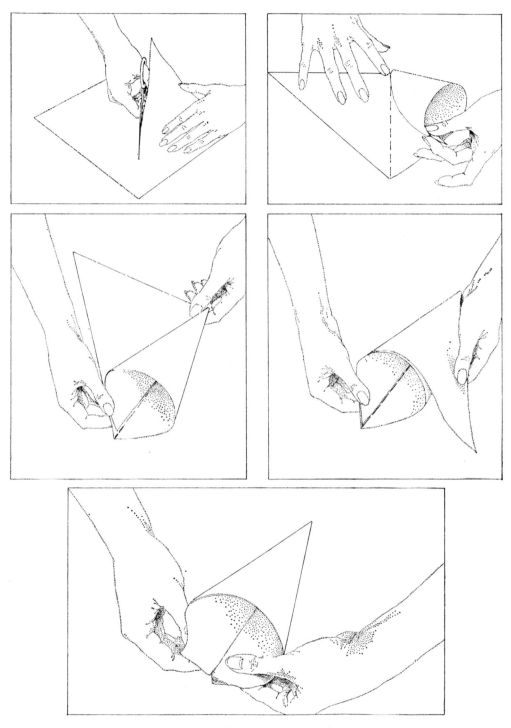

How to make your own piping bag

The first time I made a paper piping bag, I used up about a ream of greaseproof paper and about twelve hours of my time. But I'm sure you couldn't be as clumsy as I was and I didn't have me to teach me!

With the bag you've now made you can pipe a regular pattern over the top and/or sides of your gâteau or just express your inner ego with wild, indiscriminate whirls and squiggles or write some endearing or rude message on the top.

As an alternative, you can place or scatter walnuts, almonds, cashews, pecans or any other nuts, glacé cherries, whole – half or chopped – glazed orange or lemon slices or segments, angelica in strips or chopped, chopped mixed glazed fruit or a thousand and one other things – Smarties, for instance, make very effective cake decoration.

It is also most effective to have some chocolate shapes. To make these you merely melt some chocolate (the quantity depends on how many shapes you want to make and I think that plain chocolate looks and tastes better than milk chocolate), pour it evenly over waxed paper so that it forms a level sheet of chocolate and just before it is set cut it into whatever shapes you fancy with a sharp, pointed knife or an equally sharp metal pastry cutter. These shapes – dogs, cats, initials, stars, whatever they may be – can then be placed on the cake to lie flat or stuck into the cream or fondant to stand at an angle.

As you experiment you will find a thousand other 'tricks'.

Decorating Special Occasion Cakes

First of all you must trim the cake. Remove the top crust and made sure that it is absolutely flat.

Next, assuming you are using a light or rich fruit cake (see pages 102–8) pierce it several times with a pointed knife and sprinkle it fairly liberally with rum or brandy. Then cover the top and side with jam glaze (see page 120).

Now we get to the marzipan. Roll out the

marzipan on a pastry board lightly dusted with icing sugar to whatever thickness you like it to be, but not less than $\frac{1}{4}''$ or $\frac{1}{2}$ cm. Lay the cake on this top side down and trim away the marzipan that shows around it. Turn the cake back again.

Now roll the remaining marzipan into a long strip – perhaps a little thinner than for the top – at least as wide as the cake is now high and, obviously, at least as long as its circumference. Lay the cake sideways on this strip and, making sure the marzipan is sticking to the jam glaze, roll it so as to cover the sides with marzipan. With a sharp knife trim away the excess. Turn the cake back on to its base and with the flat of the hands make sure that the side and top unite. Take care not to leave finger or other indentations.

Fondant Icing (see page 130) or Royal Icing (see page 131) can now be used. The choice must be yours. Fondant is easier to use and, I think, tastes nicer. Royal icing gives a neater finish and better colours. Make your mind up and start.

To cover the cake with fondant simply pour the fondant over as with the gâteaux (see page 120) smoothing it carefully with a palette knife and put it immediately on to a cake board. Allow fondant to set completely before attempting anything further.

To cover the cake with royal icing, set it on a cake board and put this on to a turntable. (For this sort of work a turntable is almost essential.) Now, having made sure that the icing is well mixed and smooth textured, butter the top and sides of the cake with the icing using a palette knife. With practice you will be able to put a substantial blob of icing on the top of the cake, hold the edge of the palette knife at an angle to the top, spin the turntable and there you are, with enough left on the palette knife to repeat the process on the side. Sounds simple doesn't it? Persevere for a little while and you will find that it is. With royal icing it is a good idea, if you have the time, to apply a fairly thin coat first. The finish of this need not be quite perfect.

Allow it to set completely in a warm place, and then apply a further coat. Whether you use one coat or two, the final coat must be perfectly smooth. Before you can start on the artistic, decorative, fun part of decorating you must make sure that the basic icing over the cake is completely set. This may take some hours – depending on the consistency of your icing, the thickness of the coat, the temperature of the place you put the cake to set.

With both royal and fondant icing I think you will find it better to work with paper icing bags that you have made yourself than with savoy bags. The latter are rather too big for the detail that you will want; also they hold more and the contents may start setting before the bag is empty; not least important a paper bag, when finished with, is thrown away *after the piping tube has been taken out of it*, and washing a savoy bag after this particular use is a long and messy task.

The effects you can get with the various tubes that are available are endless. The results will depend on you – on *your* artistry and *your* dexterity. Again I suggest that you sacrifice some icing (fondant can be softened again if it has not set completely, royal icing can not) and practise on a metal or laminated surface. After a very short while you will find yourself looking at cakes decorated by others – professionals or enthusiastic amateurs – and working out for yourself how the various effects have been achieved.

A few general hints I can give you are:

1 Make sure your working surface is clean and dry before you start every phase of your work.
2 Make sure that all your implements and tools are clean and dry every time you use them. It is a good idea to have a deep tin of hot water by you into which to put your palette knife immediately after each use and, of course, a tea towel to wipe it dry before you use it again, and a shallow bowl of hot water for the piping tubes. If you use detergent or soap of

any kind rinse the implements thoroughly before drying them and using them again. Never, never, never let icing set on the piping tubes.

3 Before beginning to pipe icing on to your cake, squeeze some icing out through the nozzle, applying pressure at the top. This is to get rid of any air bubbles.

4 Always apply the pressure from the top.

I have left the question of colours to the end because it is the most difficult to describe though not the most difficult to accomplish. Edible, vegetable colours are available in liquid or powder form. If you are going to require quite a lot of any one colour, mix the colour into the icing in a bowl. For small quantities put a little on to a smooth working surface. Add the colour a very little at a time – it is much stronger than you think. Ensure that it is well and evenly mixed into the icing. When mixing in a bowl work the colour in thoroughly with a spatula – if fondant icing is being coloured, do this over gentle heat. If mixing a small quantity on a smooth surface use a palette knife, alternately spreading the icing and scraping it together again.

You can add a lot to the appearance and fun of a celebratory cake by putting a few models on and around it. Some of these you can buy, but it is not impossible to make models out of marzipan – practice with plasticine, anything you can make with that you can also produce with marzipan. It may be a good idea to set the marzipan in a warm place or slow oven for about half an hour. Your models can, of course, be coloured using a good water-colour brush.

The best advice I can give you, however, is get a few practical lessons from an expert. Just for the 'technical tricks'. I do not recommend a long, detailed course. It is far more fun to find out for yourself. Among the best professional decorators I have known, there was one girl who had never had a lesson in her life.

Marzipan in Cake Decoration

All cakes can be attractively embellished with marzipan shapes which, although most frequently of flowers, can be of anything that you choose to make them. It is, of course, possible to buy these shapes but, if you have the skill and the patience, it is far more satisfying to make them yourself and the best way to start is by experimenting with plasticine. When you are satisfied with your modelling in this you can move on to using marzipan.

But don't try to make this. It's simpler and less expensive to buy it at the grocer's, though it is worth buying the best, i.e. the one with the highest almond content.

Now that you are ready to try your hand at modelling with the real thing it is handy to know that if the marzipan is unmanageably hard, a little egg white will help to soften it. And, when you have made your marzipan model put it somewhere warm (like a very cool oven) to harden off – but remember, someone is going to want to eat it, so don't harden it too much. The next stage, if you have the patience for it, is the colouring of your model with good vegetable colours and a very soft brush. Your models can be realistic or fantastic – the important thing is that they should be your own creation.

Fancy Shapes in Cake Making

To make a cake in the shape of a number or letter, a heart or a horse shoe it is not necessary to spend a lot of time and money on buying suitable moulds. Make a frame the required shape – leaving about three or four inches to turn out at right-angles and fix to the baking tray with sellotape – out of cardboard! and then cover the cardboard with cooking foil which can be greased in the ordinary way. Just cut and bend the cardboard, wrap it in foil, stick it on to the baking tray, pour in the cake mix and, hey presto, you have a cake in the shape of a letter 'C'!

I am indebted to Karen Hammond, a nineteen-year-old sociology student at the University of Sussex for this ingenious method.

Some Fillings and Toppings

It is in the filling and icing of pastries and gâteaux that you will most readily be able to express your individuality and inventiveness. There is, for instance, hardly any flavour that cannot be introduced into butter cream, whipped cream or fudge filling – though I don't imagine that garlic would be very popular! The flavouring you add can be either synthetic or genuine concentrates. The latter you can make for yourself from pulped and very thoroughly strained soft fruit (raspberries, strawberries, cherries, etc.) or from the juice of citrus fruits mixed with some of the grated peel. In both cases you may find it necessary to add a drop of pure vegetable colour. I always prefer real flavours to synthetic ones. Almost any liqueur can be added to fillings and I have found that a pleasant way of adding these is by soaking dried fruit (sultanas, raisins, chopped dried apricots, etc.) in the selected liqueur overnight and then mixing these with the filling. People tell me that peppermint is a flavour rarely if ever used in pastries or gâteaux. For the life of me I cannot understand why it shouldn't be. I like a peppermint cream in a chocolate sponge. All that is needed is the addition of a very little pure peppermint oil, if you can get it – otherwise synthetic peppermint essence can be used.

I have given you only a few basic fillings and toppings – from these you can and, I hope, will develop all sorts of exciting variations of your own.

Whipped Cream Filling

1 pint (5.5 dl) whipping cream
2–4 oz (60–115 g) sugar in which vanilla pods have been standing or to which a drop or two of vanilla oil have been added

bowl – whisk

Whip the cream and sugar together until stiff enough to pipe.

NOTE: To make this into a chocolate filling just add cocoa powder to taste and possibly a little more sugar.

Fudge Filling

4 oz (115 g) soft brown sugar
2 oz (60 g) butter
1 teaspoon coffee powder
1 tablespoon golden syrup
1 tablespoon milk

saucepan – spoon – fork – teaspoon – 2 tablespoons

1 Put all the ingredients into the saucepan and bring to the boil slowly, stirring frequently but not too violently.
2 Gently simmer the mixture for 10 minutes, stirring all the time.
3 Remove from heat and allow to cool for 10 minutes.
4 Beat until you have a thick and creamy consistency.
5 Allow the filling to become quite cold before use.

Quick Blender Butter Cream

3 egg yolks
6 oz (175 g) granulated sugar
½ teaspoon vanilla essence
6 oz (175 g) butter

blender – 2 bowls – tablespoon – teaspoon – cup – spatula

1 In one bowl place half the butter and allow to soften.
2 Put the eggs, sugar and vanilla in the blender for 3 minutes.

3 Add the soft butter to the mixture in the blender until it is absorbed into the egg yolks.
4 Add the firm butter in small pieces to make the cream fairly thick.
5 Add the flavouring.

To flavour quick blended cream, stir in one of the following:

1 oz (30 g) melted unsweetened chocolate, cooled
2 tablespoons sifted dark, unsweetened chocolate powder
1 tablespoon extra strong coffee
1 tablespoon liqueur (rum, cognac, Grand Marnier, etc.)

Pastry Cream or Custard

1 oz (30 g) plain flour
$\frac{1}{4}$ pint (1.5 dl) single cream
$\frac{1}{8}$ teaspoon salt
3 oz (85 g) caster sugar
4 egg yolks
a few drops vanilla essence

2 bowls – saucepan – 2 cups – 2 tablespoons – 2 teaspoons

1 In one bowl put the flour with a quarter of the cream.
2 Add the remaining three quarters of the cream gradually and stir.
3 Place the mixture in the saucepan and stir in the salt and sugar.
4 In the other bowl stir up the egg yolks.
5 Cook the mixture in the saucepan over a medium heat, stirring until it becomes as thick as a medium white sauce. Then remove from heat.
6 Stir a little of the hot sauce into the egg yolks.
7 Pour the egg yolk mixture into the saucepan stirring briskly.
8 Return the pan to a low heat, continuing to

9

stir for a few minutes until the mixture
thickens a little more. Do not let the sauce
boil.

9 Remove from the heat and add the vanilla.
10 Cool as quickly as possible.
11 To prevent a skin forming on top of the thick
   pastry cream, while it is cooking melted butter
   may be brushed over it.
12 Stir pastry cream before using.

French Pâté Filling

*This filling is delicious for any
savoury pie or tart, or on toast. I
realise that it doesn't quite belong
among the sweet fillings but I'm
giving it anyway!*

10 oz (285 g) plain flour
4 oz (115 g) butter
1 egg
a little milk
a pinch of salt

bowl – sieve – wooden spoon

1 Sieve the flour into the bowl, making a well
  in the centre.
2 Add the milk, salt, butter and egg to the
  flour and gently stir together.
3 Knead this mixture until it becomes silky in
  texture.
4 Place in the refrigerator for $1\frac{1}{2}$–2 hours before
  using.

Fondant Icing

6 oz (175 g) caster sugar
$\frac{1}{4}$ teaspoon cream of tartar
1 egg white
3 tablespoons water

sugar thermometer – saucepan – 2 bowls – whisk
– teaspoon – tablespoon

1 Put the water in a saucepan.
2 Add the sugar and cream of tartar and dissolve
  over a low heat.

3 Bring this to boiling point (240°F/115°C) and boil for 3 minutes but do not stir.
4 Allow to cool slightly.
5 Beat the egg white until it is stiff.
6 Pour the sugar syrup in a thin, slow stream over the egg white.
7 Beat until it starts to thicken.
8 Pour the mixture quickly over the cake.

Royal Icing

1 lb (460 g) icing sugar
2 egg whites
1 dessertspoon lemon juice

2 bowls – sieve – dessertspoon – wooden spoon – whisk – spatula

1 Sieve the icing sugar into one of the bowls, making sure it is free from lumps.
2 In the other bowl whisk the egg whites to a medium stiffness, taking care not to allow it to become too stiff and form peaks.
3 Fold the whisked egg whites gently into the icing sugar.
4 Stir in the lemon juice.
5 Beat the mixture with a wooden spoon until you have a perfectly smooth, very white cream.

Uncooked Icing

1 lb (460 g) icing sugar
juice of $\frac{1}{4}$ of a good sized lemon
4 tablespoons water
colouring if desired

bowl – sieve – spoon – spatula

1 Sieve the icing sugar into a bowl.
2 Stir in the lemon juice.
3 Add a few drops of water at a time until the mixture is just thick enough to coat the back of the spoon.
4 Beat well (colouring may be added at this point if required).

Lemon Icing

4 oz (115 g) icing sugar
juice of 1 large lemon

bowl – sieve – spoon

1 Sieve the icing into a bowl.
2 Stir in the lemon juice and beat well.

Some Pastries and Ways to Use Them

Short Pastry

About the most versatile of all pastry mixes is short pastry. Petit fours, biscuits, tart cases, flan cases, pie crusts, savoury biscuits and a host of other things can be based on short pastry. With a certain amount of care it can be absolutely delicious, but beware. A little too much effort and it will be uneatable. By overworking the mix you achieve a consistency that is a blend of cardboard, rubber and concrete!

OVEN TEMPERATURE:
350°F/175°C/GAS 4
(these temperatures may vary a little depending on the use or the filling)

1 lb (460 g) plain flour
4 oz (115 g) butter
4 oz (115 g) lard
2 oz (60 g) caster sugar
1 egg
about ¼ pint (1.5 dl) cold water

bowl or pastry board – rolling pin – sharp knife – cutters, tart cases or similar

1 If you are working in a cool kitchen rub the butter and lard into the flour, taking care to produce a crumbly texture, without lumps, not a greasy dollop. Then add egg and sugar and mix them in. In a hot kitchen, however, to the extent that the fat is soft, put the butter, lard, egg and sugar into the bowl and mix them well together (mix, not beat). Then add the flour steadily, mixing as you do so.

Do not work the mixture too hard – over working will tend to make the mixture greasy and the finished article tough and 'cardboardy'.

2 Shape the mixture into a convenient shape, wrap it in greaseproof paper or cellophane and leave it to settle in the refrigerator for not less than one hour. (Note: Uncooked short pastry will keep in a refrigerator for three or four days and almost indefinitely in a freezer.)

For a slightly richer SHORT PASTRY alter the ingredients thus:

1 lb (460 g) plain flour
8 oz (230 g) butter
3 egg yolks
¼ pint (1.5 dl) cold water
2 oz (60 g) caster sugar

Follow the previous recipe in every other respect.

French Flan Pastry

There are certain things which the French have a reputation for doing better than anyone else and one of them is cooking. This French pastry is just that little bit better than ordinary short pastry – quite a big bit better in fact.

2 egg yolks
4 oz (115 g) plain flour
2 oz (60 g) caster sugar
2 oz (60 g) butter
a few drops vanilla essence
a pinch of salt

7" (20 cm) flan ring – pastry board – rolling pin – 2 bowls

1 Separate the egg yolks and whites into the two bowls.
2 Mix the flour with a pinch of salt on to the pastry board, making a well in the centre.
3 Add the sugar, butter, egg yolks and vanilla and work lightly into the flour with the tips of the fingers to make a paste.
4 Roll the paste out thinly and use as required.

Puff Pastry

It is often disasters with this delightful staple of the pastry cook's art that makes budding pastry cooks give up in despair. But, take it easy. A little time, a little effort and a little extra care will work wonders.

6 oz (175 g) butter
2 oz (115 g) lard
8 oz (230 g) plain flour
a pinch of salt
juice of half a good size lemon
cold water

sieve – bowl – palette knife – pastry board – rolling pin

1 Mix the butter and lard together and shape into a square.
2 Sift the flour and salt into a bowl.
3 Add the lemon juice and just enough cold water to make a firm dough.
4 Roll into an oblong.
5 Place the butter mixture in the centre and fold the two ends of the dough over it.
6 Seal the open ends and then roll out gently but firmly.
7 Turn through 90°, fold ends over as in step 5 above and roll out again.
8 Repeat this at least seven times, putting the

mixture into the refrigerator for a while if it becomes sticky.

9 After the final turn put into the refrigerator for at least 2 hours.

This pastry can be used for cream horns, cream slices, vol-au-vent cases, pies, tarts, palmiers, etc.

Note: When using puff pastry, always roll it out very thinly as it will 'puff' out to four or five times its original thickness.

Flaky Pastry

Like puff pastry this takes a little time and trouble but it can be done.

8 oz (230 g) plain flour
a pinch of salt
4 oz (115 g) butter
2 oz (60 g) lard
juice of half a good size lemon
cold water

sieve – bowl – palette knife – pastry board – rolling pin

1 Sift the flour and salt together into the bowl.
2 Mix the butter and lard together with the palette knife until soft and pliable.
3 Divide the fat into three equal parts.
4 Rub one part of the fat into the flour and add the lemon juice and just enough cold water to make a firm but workable dough.
5 Roll out the dough into an oblong shape about $\frac{1}{4}$" (0.5 cm) thick.
6 Divide the second part of the fat into small pieces and dot these over two thirds of the dough, lengthwise.
7 Turn the unfatted part over to cover half the fatted part and then turn the remaining part over both so that there are three layers of dough with a layer of fat between each one.
8 Turn this through an angle of 90°, seal the open edges down firmly and press the rolling pin down firmly but gently at intervals over the whole.
9 Roll out by repeated light pressure until an oblong is achieved again.

10 Repeat the fatting process (as 6, 7 and 8 above). Take care to achieve the shape by rolling and not by pulling.
11 Put in refrigerator for at least 2 hours (overnight if possible).

This pastry can be used for sausage rolls, fruit tarts, mince pies, patty cases, cream horns, etc.

Choux Pastry

Eclairs, choux buns, sweet or savoury – how versatile choux pastry is. It is also treacherous. If not made with care and affection it can end up tasting like cardboard. And even with care and affection it can prove tricky. Don't attempt it for the first time when you're having guests to dinner.

OVEN TEMPERATURE:
375°F/190°C/GAS 5

4 oz (115 g) butter
4 oz (115 g) flour
1 teaspoon salt
3, 4 or 5 eggs
1 cupful water

saucepan – bowl – whisk – 11″ × 16″ (30 cm × 40 cm) baking tray – piping bags and tubes

1 Combine the butter and water and bring to the boil over a medium heat. As soon as it is boiling reduce heat to a minimum.
2 Add the flour and salt and stir vigorously until the mixture forms a ball, then remove from heat immediately. This should take only 2 or 3 minutes.
3 Add eggs one at a time, beating each one hard. (An electric mixer should be set at three quarter speed.) After adding the second egg begin testing the mixture for consistency – it should be firm enough to form small points. Use as many eggs as you need to achieve this.
4 Put mixture into piping bag and pipe into round shapes for choux buns or long shapes for éclairs and take care to allow room for the pastries to swell up. The size of the tube depends on shape but large tubes, sizes 7, 8 or 9 will be needed.
5 Bake for about 45 minutes until there is no sign of moisture and they are pale, golden brown.
6 Turn off the oven, pierce the sides of each bun or éclair with a skewer or pointed knife and leave them in the oven for another 15–25 minutes.

When cool, the buns or éclairs may: have the top half dipped in fondant (see page 130), be filled with whipped cream (see page 127), be filled with chocolate cream (see page 128) or be filled with custard cream (see page 129).

Chocolate Pastry

Perfect your chocolate pastry, look at the fillings I suggest, invent a few more and you immediately have an impressive repertoire of exciting pastries.

OVEN TEMPERATURE:
375°F/190°C/GAS 5

6 eggs
pinch of salt
6 oz (175 g) caster sugar
6 oz (175 g) semi-sweet chocolate, melted
½ oz (15 g) coffee powder dissolved in very little water
1 teaspoon vanilla
1 oz (30 g) cocoa powder

baking sheet – 2 bowls – 2 cups – 2 tablespoons – teaspoon – fork – saucepan – whisk – spatula – sieve – waxed paper

1 Grease and line the baking sheet with waxed paper and dust with flour.
2 Separate the eggs into two bowls.
3 Add the salt to the egg whites and beat until they hold soft peaks.
4 Add the sugar, a tablespoon at a time, beating after each spoonful.
5 Beat for about 5 minutes until the mixture is very firm.
6 Stir the egg yolks with a fork to break them up.
7 Melt the chocolate in the saucepan.
8 Add the melted chocolate, coffee and vanilla to the egg yolks.
9 Fold a quarter of the stiffly beaten egg white into the chocolate mixture.
10 Pour the chocolate mixture over the remaining egg whites and fold gently together.
11 Pour the mixture into the prepared pan, spreading evenly.
12 Bake in the oven for 10 minutes, then reduce the heat to 350°F (180°C) Gas 4 and bake for a further 5 minutes or until the top of the pastry is firm.

13 Allow to cool in the pan.

14 Sieve the cocoa over a sheet of waxed paper.

15 Turn the pastry out of the pan on to the cocoa covered paper.

16 Carefully peel off the paper lining.

This can be used for: cake strips, slices and Dips (see page 52).

Pastry Cases

With flan, patty and tart cases you have the foundations for an interesting buffet. All of them can be filled with a variety of sweet and savoury fillings.

OVEN TEMPERATURE:
450°F/230°C/GAS 8

short pastry (see page 133)
uncooked rice, dried beans or dried split peas
flour to dust

rolling pin – pastry board – cutter and/or knife – fork – flan, patty or tart cases, greased

1 Roll out the pastry to a little less than $\frac{1}{4}$″ (0.5 cm) thick.

2 Cut it to fit the case you have chosen.

3 Put pastry into the case and press gently but firmly to the base and sides.

4 Pierce the base several times with the fork.

5 Quarter or half fill the case with dry rice, beans or split peas to weigh it down.

6 Bake in the pre-set oven for 10–15 minutes.

Vol au Vent Cases

For a first course, vol-au-vent cases can be filled with a great variety of fillings – fish mixtures, meat mixtures, cheese creams, vegetable mixtures etc. It is seldom done but I can think of no reason why vol-au-vent cases filled with whipped cream, custard, jam or any other sweet mixture should not be served as a dessert.

puff or flaky pastry (see pages 134–5)
1 egg
a little milk

pastry board – rolling pin – bowl – 2″ (5 cm) fluted round pastry cutter – 1″ or 1$\frac{1}{2}$″ (2.5 cm) fluted round pastry cutter – pastry brush – sharp pointed knife – or more baking sheets

1 Roll out the pastry with steady, even strokes of the rolling pin to about $\frac{1}{4}$″ (0.5 cm) thickness.

2 Cut out with 2″ (5 cm) cutter twice as many discs as vol-au-vents are required.

3 Cut the centres out of half the number of these discs with the smaller cutter, but do not remove centres.

OVEN TEMPERATURE:
400°F/205°C/GAS 6

4 Mix the egg with an equal quantity of milk to make an even liquid mixture.
5 Brush the discs with the egg wash.
6 Place the rings onto these discs, pressing down just enough to make them stick.
7 Brush over the whole with the egg wash.
8 Place on baking sheet and bake for 30–35 minutes.
9 After they have cooled, cut lightly round the inner circles of the cases to take out the top layer of the centre to form a cap for the finished vol-au-vent.

These can be filled with any number of sweet and savoury fillings ranging from jam and cream to shrimp cocktail, some of which can be served hot, some cold, some either or both. The main ingredient for the fillings is imagination!

The centres can be saved to be used as puff pastry cuttings for Cheese Straws (see below) or Sausage Rolls (see page 141).

Cheese Straws

Everyone has his own favourite recipe for these. This is mine.

OVEN TEMPERATURE:
450°F/230°C/GAS 8

puff or flaky pastry cuttings
fairly strong, grated cheese
salt

pastry board – rolling pin – sharp knife – baking sheet, greased

1 Knead the pastry cuttings together until they form one mass.
2 Roll out about $\frac{1}{4}$" (0.5 cm) thick.
3 Sprinkle liberally with grated cheese.
4 Sprinkle lightly with salt.
5 Roll the cheese in lightly with the rolling pin.
6 Cut into strips about $\frac{1}{2}$" (1.25 cm) wide.
7 Holding one end of strip steady, roll with the other hand to twist the strips.
8 Lay on the baking sheet and bake for about 10–15 minutes.
9 Cut into convenient lengths while still hot.
10 Allow to cool and crisp.

Cheese Pastry Biscuits

A little something to serve with a drink; a couple to eat with an apple for a quick snack lunch; something savoury for 'elevenses' – you could do a lot worse, and not much better, than one cheese pastry biscuit. Does that sound like an advertisement? Well, in a way I suppose that's just what it is!

OVEN TEMPERATURE:
370°F/190°C/GAS 5

1 egg yolk
8 oz (230 g) plain flour
4 oz (115 g) butter
4 oz (115 g) gruyère and/or parmesan cheese
a little salt
a little black and red pepper
a little milk

2 bowls – pastry board – rolling pin – whisk – sieve – grater – fork – baking tray

1 Separate the egg yolk into one bowl.
2 Put the sifted flour, salt, pepper and butter into the second bowl. Carefully work all the ingredients together, rubbing the butter with the fingertips until you have a breadcrumb-like mixture.
3 Take great care not to overwork the mixture as it easily becomes heavy.
4 Grate the cheese.
5 Add the grated cheese and stir gently with a fork.
6 Add a little milk to the egg yolk and mix in with the rest of the ingredients until you have a firm dough.
7 Place on a floured board and knead lightly until the mixture has a smooth texture.
8 Put the dough into the refrigerator for 30–35 minutes before rolling out.
9 Roll out to about ⅛" (0.3 cm) thickness.
10 With a knife or pastry cutter, cut into smallish shapes.
11 Place on a greased baking tray.
12 Bake in a pre-set oven for 10–15 minutes.

This dough may be used for savoury biscuits and tarts, cheese straws and canapés.

Savoury Florentines

It sometimes seems that people give drinks parties in order to invite people they don't much like. If you, however, are giving a party and inviting people you do like, why not serve some savoury florentines?

OVEN TEMPERATURE:
375°F/190°C/GAS 5

PASTRY
8 oz (230 g) puff pastry (see page 134)
1 egg yolk
FILLING
grated cheese
caraway seed
poppyseed
small knob of butter
a little salt

pastry board – rolling pin – 2″ cutter – pastry brush – bowl – cup – baking tray

1 Roll out the pastry very thinly and cut into small pieces with the cutter.
2 Brush each piece with a little of the egg yolk.
3 Sprinkle some of the centres with a little salt, some with grated cheese, some with caraway seed and some with poppyseed and put a little butter on top of each.
4 Place the pieces on a baking tray and bake until they are a golden brown colour, i.e. for about 10–15 minutes.

Sausage Rolls

Do me a favour: don't try to economise on the actual sausage meat. I won't be responsible for the damp sand effect you will surely achieve unless you observe this golden rule. Here then – using good quality sausage meat – is how to make a first-class sausage roll.

OVEN TEMPERATURE:
400°F/205°C/GAS 6

puff pastry or short pastry (see NOTE below)
1 lb (460 g) lean sausage meat, coarsely ground
3 oz (85 g) onion
1 egg, or less
a little milk
salt, pepper, ground garlic, tabasco sauce, etc., to taste

rolling pin – pastry board – sharp knife – 2 bowls – piping bag – baking sheet

NOTE: If you intend to use puff pastry it is best to use cuttings left over from some other venture. This is not just meanness. Freshly made puff pastry will expand considerably in baking and while this is fine in cream slices etc., it tends to make sausage rolls look unsightly and it also makes them awkward to eat. If you are going to use short pastry – I think short pastry is preferable here – work the pastry even less than for other uses.

1 Roll out the pastry fairly thin – less than $\frac{1}{4}''$ (0.5 cm) but not too thin to handle.
2 Cut the pastry into long strips about 3" to 4" (8 to 10 cm) wide.
3 Chop the onion very finely.
4 Mix the onion well into the sausage meat and season to taste.
5 Put the sausage meat mixture into the piping bag and pipe a strip of sausage meat along the length of each strip of pastry. (Yes, I know that piping sausage meat is hard work. The temptation to soften the mixture with a little water or milk is almost irresistible. DON'T DO IT. This would evaporate during baking and the sausage filling would shrink. It would also tend to make the pastry blow out so that you would be left with a big, ungainly roll with a comparatively small amount of filling. Some people suggest putting actual sausages into the rolls. This produces a sort of 'toad in the hole' but if you opt for this then at least take the skin off the sausage first.)
6 Dampen one edge of the strip of pastry and fold the other over the filling and pinch the two edges together well using the thumb and forefinger.
7 Score the roll lightly at about 1" (2.5 cm) intervals.
8 Mix the egg and milk to make a wash and brush over the strips.
9 Cut the strips into convenient lengths – about 3" (8 cm).
10 Place the sausage rolls on the baking sheet and bake for about 25 minutes.

Bakewell Tarts

The building of Chatsworth House was started by Sir William Cavendish in the mid-sixteenth century. Sadly he did not live to see it completed but his widow

8 oz (230 g) shortcrust pastry (see page 133)
raspberry jam
1 egg
2 oz (60 g) butter
2 oz (60 g) caster sugar
2 oz (60 g) finely ground almonds
a few drops almond essence

ensured that his dream was realised. His descendants, the dukes of Devonshire, have lived there ever since.

I don't know if the Bakewell Tart, named I suppose after the Derbyshire town of Bakewell, close by Chatsworth, has such an ancient pedigree but I do know that it is a traditional dish and like many others it is simple, subtle, wholesome and sadly underrated.

OVEN TEMPERATURE:
375°F/190°C/GAS 5

pastry board – rolling pin – 7″ (20 cm) flan tin – 3 bowls – whisk – wooden spoon – palette knife – sharp knife

1 In the first bowl make the shortcrust pastry in the usual way, then roll out the pastry and line the dish.
2 Spread a good layer of raspberry jam on top of the pastry.
3 In the second bowl whisk the eggs lightly.
4 In the third bowl cream the butter and sugar together, taking care not to over mix.
5 Add the beaten egg to the butter and sugar.
6 Still beating the mixture together, add the finely ground almonds and a few drops of the essence and mix together lightly but thoroughly.
7 Put the mixture on top of the jam and pastry, using the palette knife to spread evenly.
8 Bake in the pre-set oven for 30 minutes.

This is delicious served either hot or cold.

Congress Tarts

Political parties, trades unions, professional organisations and many other such gatherings have regular get-togethers called assemblies, conferences, conventions or congresses. This could give the Congress Tart a bad name – which it doesn't deserve!

OVEN TEMPERATURE:
325°F/160°C/GAS 3

12 oz (345g) shortcrust pastry (see page 133)
raspberry jam
3 egg whites
8 oz (230 g) caster sugar
4 oz (115 g) ground almonds
1 oz (30 g) ground rice
a little granulated sugar

pastry board – rolling pin – baking tray – 12 tart moulds 2″ (5 cm) – pastry cutter 2″ (5 cm) – 4 bowls – wooden spoon or spatula – palette knife – cooling tray

1 In one of the bowls make the shortcrust pastry (see page 133).
2 Roll this out and cut into rounds, leaving a little for the decorative strips.
3 Now, line the tart moulds with the rolled out pastry and spread a little raspberry jam in each one.

4 Separate the egg whites and yolks into two of the bowls.

5 In the fourth bowl put the caster sugar, ground almonds (which should be finely ground) and ground rice and mix carefully. Then add the egg whites and beat well with a wooden spoon or spatula.

6 Fill the tart cases with the almond mixture at least three quarters full.

7 Roll out the remaining pastry and cut into strips, using two strips for each tart so as to form a cross.

8 Dust the tops with a little granulated sugar.

9 Bake in the pre-set oven until they have a rich golden brown surface.

10 Remove from the oven and place on the cooling tray.

Redcurrant Flan

In this recipe I don't give a quantity for the redcurrants. As far as I am concerned the flan should be filled to overflowing but you can suit yourself in this.

OVEN TEMPERATURE:
Flan Pastry – 350°F/175°C/GAS 4
Meringue Top – 300°F/150°C/
GAS 1–2

FLAN PASTRY
4 oz (115 g) butter
6 oz (175 g) plain flour
2 oz (60 g) caster sugar
a little lemon juice
TOPPING AND FILLING
4 oz (115 g) caster sugar
2 egg whites
redcurrants, washed and topped

flan tin, preferably rectangular, greased and floured – fork – whisk – spatula – 3 bowls – sharp knife – sieve

FLAN PASTRY
1 Into one of the bowls put the butter and the sifted flour and rub together with the finger tips.

2 Add the sugar and lemon juice and mix together gently.

3 Put the rolled out mixture into the prepared flan tin and prick the bottom well all over with the fork, then bake in the pre-set oven until it is a light brown colour (about 15 minutes).

4 Remove from the oven and while it is still hot cover the base thickly with the prepared redcurrants and sprinkle with sugar.

TOPPING AND FILLING

1 Separate the egg yolks and whites into two bowls.

2 Whisk the egg whites until they are stiff, then whisk in half of the caster sugar, then gently fold in the remaining sugar.

3 Put this mixture on top of the redcurrants and bake in a cool oven until the meringue top has set (about 15 minutes).

4 When cold cut into slices with the sharp knife and the flan is ready to serve.

Bread

I have never met anyone who admits to liking wrapped and sliced, factory-made bread better than the crusty, flavour full, craftsman-made type, and yet sales of the former are at present many times greater than those of the latter. Something must be wrong somewhere. However, I have read that the consumption of bread in general has dropped dramatically in recent years. This could be because of the increasing pre-occupation with slimming, the increasing sophistication of taste or the increasing price of bread. Yet, as we have all observed, the little craftsman bakers nearly always have queues of eager customers and frequently sell out. Could it be . . . ? Surely not . . . ! Can the mere public assert its will on the big manufacturers?

All the same I meet more and more people who bake their own bread. Why not join them?

Consider, to begin with, your raw materials:

First and foremost there is the flour. This may be white, brown, wholemeal, granary or rye – the recipes will tell you which one is needed – and it must be fresh. Flour has a limited life – like us, it grows weaker with age – and it is worth taking the time to find a shop that has a variety of good quality, fresh flour. And having found this, buy only as much as you are going to need in the immediate future. Never attempt to store flour, even the professional bakers don't do this.

Next, there is the yeast. This can be bought 'fresh' or 'dried'. I will be honest and confess that I have never used dried yeast myself and I cannot do more than refer you to the maker's instructions on the packet which you can read as easily as I can. I can tell you, however, that yeast is a living organism and its function in bread making is dependent on its *live* activity. Despite all I have been told about how effective dried yeast is, I remain unconvinced that a living organism can be dried out, reconstituted and still work as well as it did in the first place. Throughout all the recipes in this book, cakes as well as bread, I stick to fresh yeast. This may be a little harder to find and won't keep as long but I still recommend it.

Some bread recipes also call for fat and the best one to use is pure white lard or, in some recipes, a mixture of half lard and half fresh unsalted butter. There are a number of branded cooking fats on the market which may well be pure lard but it's best to check before using them.

As for salt, which is another regular ingredient, I could be pedantic and suggest you grind your own rock salt for each occasion but I doubt whether you or I could really taste the difference that this would make. And much the same applies to sugar. The purists maintain that pure, unrefined sugar tastes better and is healthier but I am prepared to settle for the sugar in ordinary use.

A couple of general hints about method. Kneading dough is a skill that can be acquired only through experience and there are bound to be disappointments along the way. It is important, whether kneading dough by hand or by machine, to make quite sure that all the ingredients are thoroughly mixed – every one of them interacts with every other and must be given the chance to do so. The action of yeast and sugar together is a fermenting process and creates carbon dioxide gas. After the dough has risen for the first time you must be sure to work it through, re-knead it or 'knock it back', to make sure that all the bigger pockets of gas in the dough are eliminated. When you look at a slice of bread you will notice hundreds of little holes. They all once contained carbon dioxide. If you notice a great big hole then you know that someone has not done his job properly. Remember that flour contains natural sugar so this applies even in those recipes that do not call for additional sugar.

Oven temperatures and baking time may need to be varied a little. No two batches of flour are identical, the moisture content in fat may vary, yeast may be of differing ages and strength and, above all, no two ovens are identical.

To shape your bread, whether you intend to bake it on the oven bottom, on a baking sheet or in a tin, cut the amount you intend to mould (never attempt to tear it) and work it into a ball by rolling it on a *wooden* table top – marble, metal or plastic are too slippery and too cold – which has been sprinkled with flour. If a long shape is wanted roll it, by hand, from the centre to the ends with repeated steady movements. Do not try to pull it or to force it too quickly into shape. It is stubborn stuff and will shrink back. Never, never, never try to make bread in a hurry. It can't be done. If someone interrupts you while you are making bread, either invite him or her to sit, well out of the way, and watch you or ask them, politely but firmly, to go away till you are finished.

The recipes I give are just a few of the many hundreds that there are in existence. The history of bread is almost as old as the history of man and the varieties are legion. Here, for the present, are a few to be going on with.

Bread Dough (1)

OVEN TEMPERATURE:
450°F/230°C/GAS 8

3 lb (1.4 kg) plain flour
2 oz (60 g) lard
1 oz (30 g) caster sugar
1 oz (30 g) salt
2 oz (60 g) yeast
1½ pints (8.5 dl) warm water

3 loaf tins, greased – measuring jug – bowl – tea towel – bowl – pastry board – pastry brush – cooling rack.

1 Put the flour, fat, sugar and salt into the bowl

and with the tips of the fingers mix thoroughly together.

2 Pour a little of the water into the measuring jug, add the yeast and leave to dissolve.

3 Add the dissolved yeast and water to the mixture and mix well, adding more water as required, until you have a firm dough.

4 Place the dough into the pan (or another bowl) and cover with the tea towel and leave to prove in a warm place for 1 hour.

5 Remove the dough from the pan or bowl and put it onto the pastry board (or table top) and knead well, until all the gas bubbles have been expelled.

6 Return the dough, once more, to the pan and cover with the tea towel, and leave again to rise in a warm place for a further half hour.

7 Remove the dough from the pan and divide into 1 lb (460 g) pieces. Mould these into the required shapes to fit the prepared loaf tins and leave to prove, until the dough has nearly reached the top of the tins.

8 Bake in the pre-set oven until you have a firm crust on top.

9 Remove from the oven and turn out onto the cooling rack.

10 To give the bread an attractive appearance, brush the top with a little melted butter, while it is still warm.

Bread Dough (2)

OVEN TEMPERATURE:
450°F/230°C/GAS 8

2½ lb (1.15 kg) plain flour
1 oz (30 g) lard
1 oz (30 g) salt
4 oz (115 g) yeast
1 pint (5.5 dl) warm water

loaf tins, greased – bowl – seive – measuring jug – bowl – pastry board – pastry brush – cooling rack

1 Dissolve the yeast in a little of the warm water.

2 Sieve the flour into the bowl, add the cooking

fat, and rub together carefully, with the tips of the fingers.

3 Add the dissolved yeast and water to the mixture mix well adding just sufficient water to make a firm dough.

4 Repeat the same method as before in the preceding recipe.

5 Now continue the same method as before repeating the stages of the preparation of the dough shapes and place in the oven in the same way as for the previous recipe.

6 Remove from the oven and allow to cool on the cooling rack.

Cottage Loaf

OVEN TEMPERATURE:
460°F/235°C/GAS 8–9

The ingredients from either of the preceding bread dough recipes may be used for this.

round loaf tin, greased – bowl – measuring jug – tea towel – pastry board – pastry – brush – cooling rack

1 Make the bread dough according to one of the two preceding recipes.

2 When the dough is ready divide the mixture and shape into two different sized pieces. The first, for the base, should weigh 1 lb 8 oz (690 g) and the second, for the top, should weigh 10 oz (285 g).

3 Mould the pieces of dough into balls and flatten slightly, to enable the two halves to stick together.

4 Put the larger piece into the prepared loaf tin and place the smaller piece on top, press the thumb and forefinger through the centre of the top piece down through the lower piece.

5 Leave the prepared mixture in the loaf tin in a warm place to prove until it has doubled in size.

6 Bake in the pre-set oven for about 35–40 minutes.

7 Remove from the oven and turn out onto the cooling rack.

8 You may if you wish, brush the top with a little melted butter while still warm.

English Bread

OVEN TEMPERATURE:
440°F/225°C/GAS 7–8

5 lb (2.3 kg) plain flour
3 oz (85 g) yeast
2 oz (60 g) salt
a little water

baking sheet or loaf tin, greased – bowl – tea towel – pastry board – pastry brush – sharp knife – measuring jug – cooling tray

1 Put the yeast into just sufficient warm water to cover and leave to dissolve.
2 Place the flour and salt in the bowl and then add the dissolved yeast. Now add enough water to make a firm dough.
3 Cover the dough in the bowl with a tea towel, and leave it in a warm place to rise. This will probably take about an hour but depends on the room temperature.
4 Remove the dough from the bowl, onto the pastry board, and knead well until it is smooth and bubbling, then cover again with the tea towel, and leave to rise for a further $1\frac{1}{2}$–2 hours.
5 When the dough is ready it may be cut into different shapes with the sharp knife, or alternatively, shaped into one large loaf.
6 Place the shaped dough onto the baking sheet or prepared loaf tin (if making one large loaf), and bake in the pre-set oven until it is firm to touch and a golden brown in colour.
7 To test if the dough is baked sufficiently knock the bottom and it should have a hollow sound when it is well baked.
8 Remove from the oven and turn out onto the cooling rack, brush the top with a little melted butter whilst still hot.

Floris Bread

OVEN TEMPERATURE:
450°F/225°C/GAS 8

$\frac{1}{2}$ lb (230 g) finely mashed potatoes
1 lb (460 g) plain flour
$\frac{1}{2}$ oz (15 g) salt
$\frac{1}{2}$ oz (15 g) vegetable oil
2 oz (60 g) yeast
$\frac{1}{2}$ pint (2.75 dl) water

flat baking tray or sheet, greased – 2 bowls – measuring jug – cooking thermometer – cooling rack – saucepan – pastry board

1 Cook the potatoes, then strain and mash them very finely. Allow to go cold.
2 While the potatoes are cooking put the water in the saucepan and bring up to 98°c, testing this with the thermometer. Remove from the saucepan and pour the water quickly into the measuring jug, then add the yeast to dissolve in the water.
3 In the first bowl, put the flour, salt, oil and finely mashed potatoes, then add the dissolved yeast and water, and mix all these ingredients well together until you have a firm dough. Allow this to stand for 1 hour.
4 Move the dough on to the pastry board and knead or 'knock it back' (see page 147). Now mould the dough into a Coburg shape i.e. a fat sausage shape, roughly as long as it is broad. Allow the dough shapes to prove until they have doubled in size.
5 Put the dough shapes onto the prepared baking sheet and bake in the pre-set oven *with steam* for 30–35 minutes. Steam can be produced by placing a bowl of water in the bottom of the oven. This helps to give the bread a nice crispy crust.
6 Remove from the oven and place on the cooling rack.

French Bread

OVEN TEMPERATURE:
400°F/205°C/GAS 6

½ oz (15 g) yeast
a pinch of caster sugar
¾ lb (345 g) plain flour
¼ lb (115 g) brown flour
a pinch of salt
1 oz (30 g) butter
½ pint (2.75 dl) water

baking sheet (greased preferably with corn oil) – bowl – tea towel – pastry board – pastry brush – sharp knife – measuring jug

1 Put the yeast and sugar into the bowl, mix together and add the water, then gradually add the flour, butter and salt and mix all the ingredients together well.

2 Knead the mixture until it is smooth and silky in texture, then cover with the tea cloth and leave it to rise for 90–95 minutes, in a warm room.

3 When the dough has risen to double its volume, 'knock it back' and leave it to rise again for about 40–45 minutes, depending on the temperature of the room.

4 When the dough has risen sufficiently put it on to the floured pastry board and roll it out about ¼" (0.5 cm) thick, then roll it together tightly and with the hands shape into a 12" or 14" (30.5 cm or 35.6 cm) long loaf, pressing down the ends well.

5 Place the dough on the baking sheet and shape again with the hands. Now, using the sharp knife, make four or five slits about ¼" (0.5 cm) deep on the top of the dough.

6 Brush the top with a little cold water and leave it to stand for about half an hour.

7 Put the baking sheet in the pre-set oven and bake for 50 minutes, until golden brown and very crisp.

8 Remove from the oven and put onto the cooling rack.

9 This bread is delicious when eaten shortly after it has been baked.

Vienna Bread

OVEN TEMPERATURE:
450°F/225°C/GAS 8

1 pint (5.5 dl) milk
2 oz (60 g) yeast
2½ lbs (1.15 kg) plain flour
1 oz (30 g) salt
a little lard
a little malt extract

baking sheet, greased – 2 bowls – measuring jug – sharp knife – cooling rack

1 Put the milk into the measuring jug, add the yeast and allow to dissolve.

2 In the first bowl put the flour, fat, salt and malt extract, bind these together with the dissolved yeast and milk until you have a firm dough, then leave for 30 minutes to prove.

3 Knead the dough (or 'knock it back', see page 147) and leave for a further 10 minutes.

4 Weigh the dough into 8 oz (230 g) pieces and mould these into the required shapes, then place in a warm place to prove until they have doubled in size.

5 When the dough has risen score the tops with a sharp knife and place on to the prepared baking sheet.

6 The second bowl should be put into the oven with hot water in it to create steam, before placing the dough in to bake.

7 Put the baking sheet in the oven and remove the bowl of water from the oven 5 minutes later. Leave the dough on the baking sheet in the pre-set oven for 25–30 minutes to bake.

8 Remove from the oven and turn out on to the cooling rack.

Honey Bran

OVEN TEMPERATURE:
440°F/225°C/GAS 7–8

2½ oz (75 g) yeast
2 pints (1.11 l) lukewarm water
2 lb (920 g) wholemeal flour
1 oz (30 g) malt
1 lb (460 g) bran
6 oz (175 g) honey
1 oz (30 g) salt

loaf tin, greased – bowl – measuring jug – cooling rack

1 Dissolve ½ oz (15 g) of the yeast in 1 pint (5.5 dl) of water in the measuring jug.

2 In the bowl put 1 lb (460 g) of the wholemeal flour and add the dissolved yeast and water. Mix all together and leave in a warm place for at least 24 hours to ferment.

3 When the mixture has fermented and is slightly sour add the remaining 1 lb (460 g) of wholemeal flour, the bran, honey, malt and salt, then add the remaining dissolved yeast and water and mix all the ingredients together thoroughly.

4 Divide the dough into 1 lb (460 g) pieces and place in the prepared tins, then leave to prove until the dough has doubled in size.

5 Bake in the pre-set oven for 25–30 minutes.

6 Remove from the oven and turn out on to the cooling rack.

Wholemeal Bread

OVEN TEMPERATURE:
460°F/240°C/GAS 8–9

2 oz (60 g) yeast
1 pint (5.5 dl) warm water
1 lb (460 g) plain flour
2 lb (920 g) wholemeal flour
$\frac{1}{2}$ oz (15 g) oil or fat
a little salt

baking sheet or tins, greased – bowl – measuring jug – cooling rack

1 Measure the required water into the jug, add the yeast and allow to dissolve.

2 Put all the ingredients into the bowl then add the dissolved yeast and water and mix together until you have a firm dough. Allow to stand for 1 hour.

3 When the dough is ready, 'knock it back', then mould into small round shapes.

4 Place the shaped dough on to the baking sheet or tins and leave it to prove until they have doubled in size.

5 When the dough has doubled in size bake in the pre-set oven for 35 minutes or until a golden brown colour.

6 Remove from the oven and place on the cooling rack.

7 This bread is delicious if eaten as soon as it has cooled.

Austrian Rye Bread

OVEN TEMPERATURE:
440°F/225°C/GAS 7–8

1½ lb (690 g) plain white flour
2½ lb (1.15 kg) fine rye flour
2 oz (60 g) caster sugar
1½ pints (8.25 dl) water
3 oz (85 g) salt
2 oz (60 g) finely ground caraway seeds
½ oz (20 g) yeast

baking sheet, greased – bowl – small cane baskets or wooden bowls

1 Place ½ lb (230 g) of the white flour with ½ lb (230 g) of the fine rye flour in the bowl, add the sugar and mix all together with a little warm water. Allow this to stand for 24 hours in a warm place.

2 When the mixture is sour add 1 lb (460 g) of white flour, the remaining rye flour, salt, finely ground, caraway seed and the yeast, then add just sufficient warm water to make a firm smooth dough.

3 Shape the dough into small pieces and place in the greased baskets or wooden bowls and allow the dough to prove.

4 Remove the dough from the baskets or bowls and place on to the baking sheet. Bake in the pre-set oven slowly, until well baked and a golden brown colour.

5 When baked remove from the oven and turn out on to the cooling rack.

Envoi

I cannot say that this book is now complete. No cookery book ever can be, for every recipe has an infinite number of variations and every recipe inspires others. I hope that I may have given you a few ideas; I like to imagine that a suggestion of mine may have sparked off a train of thought in you that leads to what future pastry cooks will regard as a 'classic' so that I can take vicarious credit for it.

The word 'Goodbye' is a contraction of 'God be with you'. In that sense, and in that sense only, I bid you goodbye with all my heart.

Index

(Recipes are indicated in bold type)